ACCOUNTING ENGINEERING AND SPACE ACCOUNTING

İsmail Tekbaş

Translated by Sedat Üstün - kitapeditoru.com.tr

Edited by Graham Sheard - kitapeditoru.com.tr

Cover Design byYusuf Anar

ISBN: 978-1-949872-59-0

Cosmo Publishing Company

UNITED STATES OF AMERICA

Edition: February 2022

ACCOUNTING ENGINEERING AND SPACE ACCOUNTING

Two new concepts that will emerge with the digital transformation of accounting profession and the growth in space activity.

ACKNOWLEGMENTS

I would like to thank Prof.Dr Murat Azaltun, Arzu Aktaş and Ayşe Göksu Atasoy for their support.

A special thanks goes to my brother Dr Kenan Tekbas for his guidance, assistance and encouragement.

Dedicated to my wife Pınar and my daughters Öykü and Özgü.

PREFACE

Think back to when encyclopedias such as the *Meydan Larousse* and *Encyclopedia Britannica* stood as the centerpieces of our libraries. It was only 20 years ago, and they were considered our most important sources of general information. Nowadays, in the age of the internet, nobody turns to them. Professions such as shoemakers, quilt makers, tailors, and blacksmiths, all indispensable in the daily life of the past, have become outdated. And this has all happened in just the last 30 to 40 years! If anyone had come out 100 years ago and said that we could do all our shopping within just a few minutes without moving from our comfortable seats, they would have been thought of as crazy.

We have all witnessed the unprecedented speed of technological innovations in our lives. And, as an accountant experiencing the digital transformation, I now find myself asking the following questions: What will the accounting profession be like in the future? What will replace our ability to collect and record data? What hardware will we need? What kind of modeling do we need for the accounting profession to adapt to digitalization?

***

Let us turn to the global market for high technology. Here we find the global space market emerging as a macro-scale and rapidly growing sector. The international space economy, worth $423 billion[1] in 2019, is expected to increase to as much as $2.5 trillion to $3 trillion by 2024.

Of course, economic developments of this magnitude will transform the accounting profession as well. But how exactly? How important is accounting for ensuring sustainable space activities? And will we be able to solve accounting problems generated by space exploration with traditional accounting methods?

---

1 2019 Space Foundation Report www.thespacereport.org/pricing

***

This book centers around two concepts. The first is the concept of **accounting engineering**, which was introduced into the literature after the 2nd International Thrace Accounting, Finance and Auditing Symposium, held on October 18, 2017. The other is the concept of **space accounting**, which was first cited at the 4th International Accounting and Finance Research Congress, held on October 23–25, 2019.

The concepts of accounting engineering and space accounting are steps taken in the name of change and transformation for the accounting profession as a whole. My aim is that this book will shed some light for my colleagues who are curious about the questions mentioned above, and that it will inspire them to implement any insights into other projects.

We are on the edge of change comparable to the rise of human life on Earth.

Vernor Vinge

ABBREVIATIONS

ACA : associate chartered accountant (qualified with ICAEW)
ACCA : Association of Chartered Certified Accountants
AICPA: American Institute of Certified Public Accountants
ASO : Ankara Chamber of Industry
AR : augmented reality
CAAP : computer-aided audit project
BCI : brain computer interface
ISC : information society department
ISS : information society strategy and action plan
SPO : state planning organization
OEI : other earnings and incomes
CRM : customer relationship management
E-STATEMENT: electronic statement
EC : European Commission
ERP : enterprise resource planning
EU : European Union
EUROSTAT : European Union Statistical Institute European Statistics Office
E-LEDGER : electronic ledger
E-INVOICE : electronic invoice
SWOT : strengths / weaknesses / opportunities and threats
ICR : intelligent character recognition
ICAEW: Institute of Chartered Accountants in England and Wales
ICT : information and communication technology
IES 2 : professional accounting education programs
IoT : internet of things
IFAC : International Federation of Accountants
MDGs : millennium development goals
PwC : PricewaterhouseCoopers
RFID : radio frequency identification
RPA : robotic process automation
UN : United Nations
UN DESA : United Nations Department of Economic and Social Relations
USA : United States of America
WB : World Bank

CONTENT

LIST OF FIGURES

LIST OF TABLES

INTRODUCTION

In the 1990s, in Hollywood's blockbuster science fiction movies, the twenty-first century was imagined as a time of robots trying to take over the world, flying cars, artificial intelligence computers, and technological conflict. Some of these predictions have already come true less than 30 years later. From driverless cars to autonomous call centers, from unmanned dark factories to self-learning machines… They have manifested, with new technological developments being added to the list every day.

The struggle between machine and man is as old as the invention of the wheel. Nowadays, the big fear is not that robots are taking over the world, but that they are taking jobs away from large communities of people! Of course, accounting is one of the professions where this fear is most felt.

Terminator, Star Wars, Star Trek, Back to the Future, and The Matrix were among the most popular science fiction movies of the 1970s, 1980s, and 1990s.

Even very old handwritten documents can be digitized by scanning and saving them on to a computer. The digital world collects, transforms, and stores the information and then provides easy access to it. With the internet, cloud technology, big data, and artificial intelligence (AI), all our information is shifting to digital platforms and becoming more and more automated. The digital world has evolved continually in terms of legislation, technology, tactics, and user experience, and it continues to evolve at an increasing pace.

It should not be too long before the emergence of self-learning AI accounting programs that can work 24 hours a day, 365 days a year, without interruption, and without making a single mistake. It is both annoying and exciting that accounting processes can be performed better by these advanced programs. In this new world, the use of technology for manual and routine accounting not only saves time for accountants but also dramatically reduces human error. By keeping routine and ordinary records in this way, accountants are allowed to turn to more value-added tasks, such as data science, consulting, analysis, interpretation, system design, strategy, and auditing.

In summary, the Fourth Industrial Revolution has brought about developments in artificial intelligence, robotic technologies, cloud systems, blockchain, and digitalization, and these advances have created the need to redefine the accounting profession. New technologies are changing both our application processes, and the skill sets we will need. In particular, they will radically alter the costs, speed, and accuracy of accounting applications. We are at the beginning of a new and exciting era for the accounting profession – and the need to address this is urgent.

***

Digital transformation is a profound transformation of people and society in all aspects. It provides an intersection point between science and engineering applications and the arts and human sciences. This period of transformation is also marked by the use of digital technologies to make processes more efficient or effective. The objective is not only to digitally replicate an existing service but also to use the technology to significantly improve that service. It does this by responding to the transformation process, as it redefines and analyzes old processes and organizations. This ability to create alternatives and to imagine a better future makes it strategically important.

But it is not only about imagining Utopias that may predict a possible future; digital transformation also represents a way of keeping alive the data literacy and fluency that it has brought to many aspects of our social and personal lives, while foreseeing meaningful and profound changes in the short term.

With all this in mind, we can ask the central question of this book: **What is the future of the accounting profession in the age of digital transformation?**

Throughout history, many old ways of working have disappeared over time, and it would be impossible to find accountants today who use the traditional method of just paper and pencil. With digitalization, many professions are being forced to reinvent themselves or are disappearing altogether. Just as automatic elevators removed the need for the elevator operators of the past, automation systems have now begun to replace cashiers, truck drivers, and baristas. E-commerce sites are taking the place of stores. Interestingly, technology will sometimes create whole new classes of profession that can replace those becoming outdated.

Digital transformation opens up the future of the accounting profession by forcing a re-examination of current practices. It is now crucial that accountants acquire the new skills that information technology demands. Government agencies around the world are taking steps to implement technological advancements in the quest to prevent an unregistered economy while also reducing expense items, such as staff, time, and paper. To achieve this, they are investing in information technologies and automation systems (such as e-invoice and e-ledger).

The Fourth Industrial Revolution, also known as Industry 4.0, is causing the most significant transformation of the accounting profession since our transition to the double-entry accounting system in the fifteenth century. Revolutions always have devastating consequences as well as positive results, and the digital revolution is no different. It directly affects people's lives, eliminating some of their skill sets, and making it necessary to replace them with new ones. It will mean certain materials and methods, such as paper, receipts, manual recording, declaration, and notification, will be discontinued and probably replaced by barcode systems and internet-based accounting (cloud system and blockchain technology). The definition of accounting, and the duties of accountants, will change, and so will businesses' expectations of them.

As experts in this business, we must be ready to provide value-added jobs such as consultancy and system design. It takes more than technical accounting knowledge to be successful in the digital age. Accountants of the future must be able to think strategically, communicate effectively, and they must know technology in order to uncover the opportunities that can be created for accounting. Therefore, it is critical to restructure the accountancy profession, to re-determine the competencies of accountants, and to cultivate forward-looking ideas on this issue.

In my opinion, accountants will have to combine their existing theoretical and practical knowledge with mathematical, philosophical, and engineering skills, in parallel with technological developments. Engineering skills, for example, will be required to correct analysis and interpretation of large and diverse data produced by digital systems. Technological developments will force the accounting profession to radically change and transform within the digital transformation framework in areas such as education, culture, and practice.

So, how can we adapt to this digital transformation? As with previous revolutions, there is likely to be confusion. Business models and industries are transforming faster than ever before.

***

What do we need for digital transformation? The best answer I can give is "design-oriented thinking". Design-oriented thinking offers the tools (logical thinking, creativity, and reasoning) that you need in the transformation process. It provides a wealth of ideas in terms of disciplines and perspectives. The most crucial opportunity it offers is its contribution to solving major problems. The accounting profession needs radical change in order to be more innovative. The driving force behind transformation and evolution can only be design. Therefore, it is necessary to look at accounting engineering with this in mind.

Engineering has been transformed into a profession over time and is based on thought systematics. It prioritizes thinking abilities and is not solely concerned with the design and construction of buildings, machines, or systems. It is also involved in many social and global problems, such as poverty, inequality, disaster recovery and climate change. New concepts such as social engineering, change engineering, and risk engineering are developing approaches in the engineering discipline.

Accounting engineering aims to transform the accounting profession in the fields of thought, education, culture, and technology. It seeks to redesign the competencies of accountants within a framework of engineering capabilities in conjunction with digitalization.

Accounting engineering will provide accountants with a newly designed career field. They will be people who have the skills to design systems, analyze and interpret big data correctly. They will also be able to define accounting problems, produce scientific solutions to these problems, re-design the financial structure of enterprises for their financial future, and develop new strategies.

A major transition to a new accounting model requires fundamental change. Of course, this will not happen overnight. In order to ensure such a transformation, the accountant candidates' technological infrastructure must be prepared – and this can only be achieved through education reform.

In many countries, traditional accounting education lacks the course content designed for critical thinking, problem-solving, scientific thinking, decision-making, and analytical thinking, which are among the most critical skills required for accurate analysis and interpretation of digital and big data. However, acquiring these skills is a must for tomorrow's accounting leaders.

The basic strategy of accounting engineering – which I aim to see established as a profession and as a new education department in universities – is to redesign accounting education, taking into consideration the technological developments and the skills required by the twenty-first century. You will find a detailed clarification of this concept in the following sections.

CHAPTER I
CONCEPTUAL FRAMEWORK AND HISTORICAL DEVELOPMENT OF ACCOUNTING

A photograph of accounting staff in bygone times. There is no trace of this image in accounting today.

Accounting is a profession that came into existence spontaneously, to respond to the needs and necessities of daily life. It can be defined as an information system that records, classifies, summarizes, and reports the financial transactions and events of enterprises. It then interprets and communicates the results back to them. Since accounting is concerned with the nature of any basic information that allows the planning, execution, and supervision of an enterprise's activities, it empowers business owners and managers to make good, informed decisions. In this framework, it is considered the language of business – and it is obviously essential to use understandable language when presenting information.

As a system of information, accounting explains the formation of the assets and resources of enterprises, the manner of their use, and the increases and decreases in their worth them as a result of financial transactions. In other words, it identifies the assets and resources owned by an enterprise. The financial results that emerge become understandable by examining the activities of the enterprises during the relevant financial period.

In addition to this, accounting identifies and presents certain economic situations in businesses and can provide evidence in possible legal disputes with third parties. Thus, it protects the assets of the enterprise against misuse by operating personnel. It also calculates the taxes that businesses are liable to pay and provides the financial data that business managers need in their decision-making to ensure continuation and/or growth.

The results of the accounting system are created from the observance of certain principles and rules. These rules, principles, and regulations are agreed upon by professional standards boards and this is what ensures accounting is held to a certain standard. Accounting results must be comparable, verifiable, and impartial, and the data should be reliable since it is based on external sources and documents.

Traditional accounting practices are based on well-established standards and systems. However, this conventional structure is now lagging and will face significant changes in the next decade. As technology increases and intelligent innovations transform the sector, some of the basic concepts and functions of the accounting profession will become obsolete. For example, when data is generated automatically by digital systems, the recording, classification, and summarizing functions of accounting will lose their validity. Accounting is still about numbers, but now it goes beyond reporting these numbers to provide information. Advancements in technology are reshaping accounting's traditional role: accountants are becoming increasingly dependent on mobile devices to access data, and their expertise is evolving beyond registration, reporting, and tax services and moving into strategic consulting.

The fact that virtual currencies will replace money, bonds, and checks in the future will cause the basic concepts of accounting to change. In particular, digital systems will automate data collection more fully, while also increasing data quality and reducing data validation time. With business analysis services such as Microsoft Power BI, accountants can create their reports and indicator tables more easily, and this new process can significantly automate tax/legislation work and the more labor-intensive parts of accounting.

With accountants using increasingly sophisticated and intelligent technologies to improve and even replace their traditional ways of working, it is now a necessity to review the profession in a radical manner and revise its definition and functions.

Globalization will provide more opportunities for accountants; however, it will also bring the challenge of ensuring they have sufficient digital technology training. Professional organizations and educational institutions will have to respond to this challenge. Unfortunately, education curricula are not yet in line with the future needs of accounting students. Despite the efforts made by professional accountants and academic researchers, there is a surprising gap in research on the changes that could affect those in the accounting profession. Accounting institutions need to cooperate with universities to open new departments in such subjects as cloud informatics, big data, digitalisation, digital transformation, and integrated reporting. Universities need to invest in training existing faculty members on digital transformation and in employing new experts to coordinate these new units and give lectures. In summary, the sustainability of accounting should be placed at the very center of education and training.

For hundreds of years, accountants have been responsible for the accuracy of tax payments. They have generated value by interpreting this data to help business owners make better decisions. Now, the profession must prepare for the future by adapting to the ongoing change and transformation that we are already experiencing.

I.1-ACCOUNTING PROFESSION

We need to go back at least 7,000 years to ancient Mesopotamia to understand why accounting has made such an impact on our lives. This is the age that historians think accounting first emerged as a professional concept. The oldest accounting artefacts to have been found date back to this civilization, and it is believed that writing was first used by the Sumerians in Mesopotamia (4000–2000 BCE) for recording purposes in the storage processes of agricultural products. Certain unearthed Sumerian inscriptions contain grain and sheep-like shapes symbolizing agrarian products. It is thought that the world's first accountants worked for temples, assessing taxes paid on sheep and agrarian products for the religious authorities.

Religions, governments, and various institutions have had a big impact on the emergence and development of the concept of accounting, and this concept has changed significantly over time. In his book *Accounting Theory*, Alfred Isaac explains: "In the past, accounting was considered equal to bookkeeping. However, in today's economy, some records have also emerged other than those used in bookkeeping; the concept of accounting has gradually expanded." Accounting continued its development in the historical process and became a profession over time. People who fulfilled the duties of accounting, who acted as brokers in the achievement of stated goals and results, and who carried out this profession, were then called "accountants".

The profession is now practiced in a wide range of fields, and accountants are key players in many aspects of business life. However, accounting is not only a fundamental component of economic and commercial development, but also essential for the sustainability of life. For this reason, accountants must perform their duties accurately and completely.

The accounting profession is based on two key features: expertise and responsibility. The accountant knows what they must do, how they will do it, and why they will do it. They should make the correct diagnosis and present the right advice and solutions. Most importantly, they should comply with the profession's ethical principles of honesty, reliability, transparency, impartiality, independence, and social responsibility.

Accountants are invaluable for businesses. They examine companies' financial information with an inquisitive mind, and their training enables them to adopt a pragmatic and objective approach to solving problems. They give companies advice, helping them to achieve their goals and to reduce their costs and risks, and they represent the interests of the company. Their role includes creating, communicating, and analyzing financial information to manage the organization, while establishing and maintaining the strategic direction of the business.

As internal auditors, accountants provide assurance on whether the organization's risk management and internal control processes are working effectively or not. Accountants in the public sector shape fiscal policies that affect the lives of many people. And those in an academic environment undertake the role of transferring the profession's knowledge, skills, and ethical foundations to new generations.

Accountants perform indispensable tasks for individuals, businesses, public institutions, and organizations, and more importantly, for governments. They operate within a framework that's affected by changes in society and in national economic structures, and they are expected to meet the information needs of information users as well as investors accordingly.

As technology has developed, so has the ability of accountants to analyze and interpret statistical figures. This progress, which started with the invention of the abacus, advanced rapidly in the twentieth century as information systems and computers took over from calculators, notebooks, and pens. Future versions of accounting applications will determine which jobs we perform in the twenty-first century (as will increasing assistance from artificial intelligence accounting programs).

The proliferation of systems in the accounting profession, particularly mobile and cloud technology, increases productivity, facilitates customer relationships, and offers accountants new opportunities to expand their services. Mobile devices are becoming accounting firms' most critical tools. Equipped with numerous applications and cloud-based solutions that can make complex financial calculations easier, they can also be used as portable handheld scanners for client documents. Thus, accountants can now provide services to their clients from virtual offices whenever and wherever they want.

As technology advances, accountants can (eventually) turn to business information analysis consulting, delivering further value to their executive clients and meeting their higher expectations. For accounting professionals to understand the future, they need to have a global perspective and keep up with the changes in technological advancements.

I.2-HISTORICAL DEVELOPMENT OF ACCOUNTING PROFESSION

In his book *Sapiens: A Brief History of Man from Animals to Gods*, Yuval Noah Harari says: "The first texts in history were not documents that mentioned a philosophical thought, poetry, legend, law, even victories of war but they were economic documents about tax payments, debt accumulation, and property ownership. It is significant that the first person whose name was written in history was an accountant rather than a prophet, poet, or great commander."[2]

Most accounting historians believe writing and numbers were born of the accounting (reckoning) needs of the people. Such claims indicate that accounting existed even before the invention of writing. I believe that more accounting evidence may even be found in the ongoing excavations at Gobeklitepe (Upper Mesopotamia/modern-day Turkey), which dates back 7,500 years earlier than the oldest known accounting artefacts so far (which themselves caused world history to be rewritten).

Table1. Accounting in Sumerians: The duality principle

Principle of duality		
Cost of production of goods and services	**Equals**	**Variation of the equity component (inventory of the temple)**

Source: Provasi and Farag, 2013

The oldest known accounting records are from Mesopotamia around 7,000 years ago. The Mesopotamians kept many records using extremely durable clay tablets. These tablets, produced over a long period between approximately 5000 BCE and 2500 BCE, provide us with a unique insight into Mesopotamian civilizations and history

2 Harari, Y. N., & Genk, E. (2015). Sapiens*: A Brief History of Humankind*, Vintage

– and of course accounting records have an important place among them.

Traded goods are listed in many of the Mesopotamian documents. Transaction records are short but detailed, and most of the content of legal records relates to accounting. Accountants not only had to keep track and produce the records, but they also had to make sure that contracts were compliant with the rules. The tablets form a fairly standard database, but what is interesting is how the Mesopotamians obtained this data and used it for various accounting purposes, such as management and decision-making. Records were used for administrative procedures, registration of legal and sacred traditions, preparation of annual budgets, and the recording of scientific events.

In archaeological excavations of the Mesopatamian civilizations of Babylon (1894–539 BCE), Assyria (*c.*2500–609 BCE), and Sumer (*c.*4000–2000 BCE), it was discovered that primitive accounting methods were used to record the growth of crops and flocks. This means accounting could be considered the oldest management technique.

Historians believe the origins of the accounting profession lie in an area extending from the Nile valley in Egypt to the Euphrates and Tigris rivers in Mesopotamia. Writing and arithmetic were necessary for the advancement of accounting – but so were writing materials. Papyrus in the Nile valley and clay tablets in the Euphrates and Tigris valleys were used for this purpose. Finding the first traces of accounting in these regions directly relates to the fact that the first traces of civilization are found in these regions. Civilization brought with it the development of commercial relations and the economy – and this in turn created a need to keep records.

The Egyptians were never able to go further than simple accounting records, but they had the significant advantage of being able to use papyrus instead of clay, and their records were more detailed than the Mesopotamians' as a result. Every Egyptian accountant had a role and a specific warehouse for which he was responsible. The records were kept meticulously and diligently because those found to have false records could be punished with fines, torture, and even death.

Between 4000 BCE and 3000 BCE, Iranian kings and priests oversaw the people on financial matters. Cylinder symbols were used for accounting on the clay tablets found in this region. Buildings with large rooms were found that were used for the storage of crops. These findings included graphical representations, and this discovery represented a major scientific leap for accounting.

During the first millennium BCE, the spread of trade increased the role of the accountant. The Phoenicians invented a phonetic alphabet for bookkeeping, and in Egypt someone was recorded as being the "head of writing". By the 4th century BCE, the Egyptians and Babylonians had established inspection systems to control movement in warehouses, including spoken "audit reports".

During the Roman era (27 BCE–395 CE), accounting records were kept for all financial transactions, including land and money grants to the public, public expenditures, temple constructions, theater performances, and gladiator games. Roman emperors used accounting information to plan, control, and make decisions. In addition, transaction records, on cash and commodities for example, were kept meticulously by the Roman army. The "Title Deeds of the Divine Augustus" contains the financial relations of the Roman emperor Augustus. Public expenditures covering a period of 40 years were listed in inscriptions during his rule, approximately 2,000 years ago.[3] Although the eventual collapse of the Roman Empire meant Roman accounting also collapsed, several important accounting methods were later preserved by the bishops of Rome right through to the Renaissance.

The ancient Indian philosopher and economist Chanakya wrote a kind of financial management book called *Arthashastra* at some point during the Mauryan Empire of 322–185 BCE. The book contained several detailed points on maintaining accounting ledgers for a sovereign state.

---

3 Oldroyd, David (1995) "Role of accounting in public expenditure and monetary policy in the first century AD Roman Empire," *Accounting Historians Journal*: Vol. 22: Iss. 2, Article 5.

Much later, more sophisticated records became necessary for accounting due to business developments in the thirteenth century. This demand led to the first move towards a modern-accounting double-entry system of records. In primitive accounting (a simple registration system), where financial transactions were expressed with a single record, it was easy to make mistakes but difficult to find the errors. In the double-entry accounting system, financial transactions began to be recorded at least twice. This system reduced the possibility of making mistakes and made it easier to detect them.

The double-entry accounting system – which would become obligatory with the development of Mediterranean trade during both the medieval Crusades and the commercial revival of the Renaissance – was first pioneered in around 1299-1300 in Florence by Del Bene, a company operating in the import, production, and clothing trades.

In the fourteenth century, Italian merchants had begun to set up multiple branches as their economic activities grew. Together with the first banks, they obtained greater control over the regulation of all trade from Italy to Central Asia. This advancement enabled Italian merchants to be economically and politically influential in lands stretching from Scandinavia to India. In 1340, the city administration of Genoa implemented an account plan in which they used the city account as a capital account, with a double-entry accounting system. This accounting plan required the expense and income accounts to be closed at the end of each year.

A significant improvement was made in the double-entry accounting system with the records of Francesco di Marco Datini, who was engaged in trade and banking. Datini moved from the single-entry to the double-entry accounting system in 1390. For his balance sheet, he added concepts such as debtors, creditors, foreign receipts balance, balance of branches, inventory, doubtful receivables, taxes payable, depreciation, reserves, share certificates, and errors that cannot be traced in the arrangement of the balance sheet. The Medicis, another well-established family of Florence, also made significant developments in this regard with the bank they established in 1397. They opened important branches in other cities in Italy, considered each branch a separate entity, and prioritized the control of accounts between branches.

Western accounting historians have widely accepted that the first book written on accounting was *Summa de Arithmetica Geometria Proportioni et Proportionalita*, written in 1494 by the Italian mathematician and monk Luca Pacioli.[4] His book was an instruction in standard mathematics, but an entire chapter, titled "*De Computis et Scriptures*", was about accounting, and this was later published as a separate book in Tuscany under the name *La Scuola Perfetto dei Mercanti* in 1504. Pacioli is sometimes considered the father of accounting because of these books but, in fact, the accounting methods he described had already been used in Venice for some 200 years.

Although *Summa* is often cited as the first accounting book, Abdullah Ibn Muhammed Ibn Kiya AI-Mazanderani wrote detailed information and examples about the double-entry accounting system in his work *Resalâ-i Falakiyya der ilmi Siyagat* in 1363 – a good 131 years before Pacioli. According to AI-Mazanderani, ledgers, recording methods, documents, and accounting types have an essential place in the accounting of nations.[5] He stressed the importance of accounting for both state and society, and claimed it was more honorable than other sciences. He also argued that state affairs would not be able to function unless there were accounting transactions, and that the financial structures of states might deteriorate if income-expense records were not carried out correctly.

The simple accounting system described by Pacioli was widely used in fifteenth century Italy – so much so that by the middle of that century, the Del Bene company was using two accounting registers: one dedicated to cost records and the other to business transactions. Although Pacioli did not mention it in his book, cost analysis forms were already in use during his lifetime, and Datini had used separate columns for foreign currencies in his accounting, even calculating the

4 Ovunda, A. S. (2015). Luca Pacioli's Double-Entry System of Accounting: A Critique. *Research Journal of Finance and Accounting, 6*(18), 132-139.

5 Can, A. V. (2007). Luca Pacioli Muhasebenin Babasi midir? *Akademik Bakis, Uluslararasi Hakemli Sosyal Bilimler Dergisi*, (12).

profit and loss resulting from the difference between domestic and foreign currency values.

The beginnings of double-entry accounting in Europe in the Middle Ages established the foundation of financial reporting for businesses around the world. By the 1500s, accounting was not just a trade practice in Europe; it also attracted the attention of those who were interested in religion, art, and philosophy. They considered good accounting the key to their assets and to the moral health of society – so much so that accounting was often depicted in European artistic works of the period. In Jan Provost's painting *Death and the Miser*, there is a representation of the glory of accounting itself, and not just of wealth and financial success. French painter Jan Gossaert poetically showed a merchant writing a couplet about the corporate report in his *Portrait of a Merchant*. The Europeans not only dominated world trade in the fifteenth century, but they also depicted themselves doing so in hundreds of paintings, and accounting tables and symbols often featured.[6]

Many books on accounting were published in various languages throughout the sixteenth century. Domenico Manzoni's book *Quaderno doppio col suo giornale secondo il costume di Venetio* was published six times between 1540 and 1574, but some parts of the book were pure excerpts from Pacioli's book. The first English accounting book was Hugh Oldcastle's *Profitable Treatyce*, published in 1543. Like Manzoni's work, it cited Pacioli verbatim.

In 1769, Benjamin Booth proposed the use of a sub-ledger before passing it on to the ledger. The double-entry accounting system was already widely used in England and some parts of the Netherlands and Europe during the sixteenth and seventeenth centuries, but it began to be discussed and developed in the eighteenth century. With the help of the information contained in those first books on accounting, the practitioners of the period – such as Benjamin Booth – played a major role in developing the recording and reporting methods used today.

---

6 Soll, J. (2014). The vanished grandeur of accounting: Once, bookkeepers were valorized in great art. Sound funny now? The joke might be on us. *The Boston Globe, 8*.

Josiah Wedgwood was best known for his outstanding work in the pottery and ceramics industry in the eighteenth century, but he is also considered to have been the first cost accountant.[7] Records from 1772 show he made great efforts to generate the profit or loss of each product he sold, taking into account the cost of materials and labor, and the expenses for coal, storage, and transportation.

The Industrial Revolution, and the consequent emergence of joint-stock companies, large-scale production, more extensive competition, and the desire to maximize profit, created new problems and complexities in the state-controlled accounting system. The accounting analysis process emerged to solve these problems and complexities, and it was during this period that European accounting writers produced the fundamental theories that made the accounting system more logical.

The form of modern accounting that we use today developed in the nineteenth century due to developments in Scotland. Until this point, accountants and lawyers operated within the same associations, and lawyers sometimes even offered accounting services themselves. In 1854, however, 49 accountants in Glasgow successfully submitted a petition to Queen Victoria for the creation of an Institute of Accountants of Scotland (ICAS). The petition stated that accounting was a respected and long-standing profession in Scotland. Although the number of practitioners was small at this time, their numbers were increasing.[8]

At around the same time, the Industrial Revolution gathered pace in England, and London became the world's financial center. With the emergence and growth of limited liability companies, demand increased for technically competent accountants who could respond to the increasingly complex world of high-speed global transactions and large-scale manufacturing and logistics, and who could

---

7 Dodgson, M. (2011). Exploring new combinations in innovation and entrepreneurship: social networks, Schumpeter, and the case of Josiah Wedgwood (1730–1795). *Industrial and Corporate Change*, *20*(4), 1119-1151.

8 Lee, T. A. (2013). Reflections on the origins of modern accounting. Accounting History, 18(2), 141-161.

calculate figures such as asset depreciation and inventory valuation. Accordingly, accountants had to be aware of the latest technology.

As companies grew, accountants became an integral part of the business and financial system. To improve their situation and to combat low standards, local professional organizations in England established the Institute of Chartered Accountants in England and Wales (ICAEW) in 1880 by royal charter. Mary Harris Smith became the world's first certified female accountant and was admitted to ICAEW in 1919.[9]

The gradual development process of the accounting system after 1950 is called the "modern period". After World War II, the production system changed drastically due to extraordinary advances in science and technology. Considerable progress was made in industry and trade, and life changed dramatically, both economically and socially.

Today, millions of accountants work all over the world and serve hundreds of thousands of organizations. It's not exaggerating to say that it's thanks to accountants that the wheels of the economy spin. They may not be solely responsible, but they certainly play a significant part. Every business, every company, every government, and even every individual uses at least some basic accounting principles in their daily activities.

9 https://www.icaew.com/library/historical-resources/female-firsts

I.3-TECHNOLOGICAL EVOLUTION OF ACCOUNTING

The impact of technological developments on society and their potential to fundamentally shape human evolution are among the hottest topics for scientific research.

Humans lived as hunter-gatherers for millions of years until, around 10,000 years ago, they learned to grow crops and domesticate animals and eventually became an agricultural society. The Industrial Revolution of the eighteenth and nineteenth centuries created a new industrial society. Today, we are moving from an information society to a digital society. Technology arguably forms the basis of all these evolutionary steps, and technological developments create an evolutionary process for all living and even non-living things. In recent years, concepts and principles have been borrowed from evolutionary biology to try to describe and explain technological progress.

Although the development and structure of accounting are influenced by numerous factors, such as the economy, culture, globalization, politics, and governments, it is helpful to systematically examine the historical evolution of accounting from a purely technological perspective.

The accounting profession is not static but dynamic, and new combinations of applications and processes are continually built over old ones as it keeps up with technological developments. Throughout its historical development, the accounting process has evolved from a primitive, inconsistent, and confusing state to a disciplined system; from clay tablets to accounting software; from single data entry to advanced accounting standards. It has become much more complicated over time. So, do new technological developments such as artificial intelligence, blockchain, big data, and cloud systems reveal an evolutionary process in accounting?

Accounting and technology are in constant interaction. Without an abacus, calculator, computer, printer, and accounting programs, it would not be possible for accounting to have reached its present level. We cannot say that accounting has developed entirely as a result of technology, but it may well be claimed that technology has created an evolutionary process for accounting. For example, paper invoices evolved from being prepared manually to being issued via accounting programs to being issued digitally as e-invoices today. The e-invoice did not emerge suddenly out of nowhere; it came into being through the evolution of the paper invoice. The same is true for other applications of accounting: each was created when the applications that preceded them changed with the impact of technology.

What benefit is there in saying that the changes and transformations in accounting are a technological evolution? This perspective can help us to understand the role of technological innovations in the changes in accounting and can indicate how we can implement such innovations successfully. An approach that considers the technological evolution of accounting may be especially helpful in answering critical questions posed by digitalization, such as: “Will the accounting profession disappear?” and “Will artificial intelligence systems replace accountants?”

Accounting will not disappear with digitalization, but it will undergo a transformation. The necessary competencies of accountants will change and it’s crucial that accounting education adapts accordingly.

Technology and Evolution

The theory of evolution by natural selection, put forward by Charles Darwin in 1859, was developed to explain observations regarding the transformation of living things, and the emergence and evolution of new species. The theory, published in his book *On the Origin of Species,* made people question their place in the world. Four years later, writer Samuel Butler called for a theory of evolution for machines. He claimed that Darwin’s principles of evolution could be used not only for biological processes, but also for the analysis and explanation of technological change and innovation in machinery.

In his 1988 book *The Evolution of Technology*, science historian George Basalla claimed that all technological innovation, including seemingly brand-new achievements, actually came into being by synthesizing or modifying existing technologies. He argued that every technological innovation was affected by the technologies before it, and that the Industrial Revolution was actually an industrial evolution.

Economic historian Joel Mokyr has also presented an evolutionary theory of technology that focuses on the development of technological knowledge and agrees that evolutionary biology provides a useful analogy or metaphor. His objective is to develop an evolutionary framework that helps analyze the root causes of technological change.[10]

Technology's evolutionary process has directly impacted on the evolutionary process of accounting applications. How accounting has been shaped and developed over the centuries, from the ancient Egyptians' use of papyrus for recording purposes to today's cloud systems is a good case in point. But is accounting itself evolutionary or revolutionary? It is necessary to create a new approach or paradigm for radical models. Evolutionary models, on the other hand, are based on redesigning or transforming existing models. The theory of evolution and systems theory can help us to understand the technological dynamics behind the changes in the accounting profession.

The historical changes in accounting over time show that it is in the process of non-instantaneous, uninterrupted, qualitative, and quantitative development. This development, which began with the invention of clay tablets and papyrus, reached the level of computers and accounting software in the twentieth century. In the twenty-first century, we expect artificial intelligence and blockchain technologies to digitalize the functions and applications of accounting. Technology directly shapes the accounting profession, and technology is the basis of modern accounting.

According to Darwin, evolution is the result of adaptation to the environment and natural selection. Creatures living in different

---

10 BREY, P. (2008), Technological Design as an Evolutionary Process." Eds. Vermaas, P., Kroes, P., Light, A. and Moore, S. Philosophy and Design: From Engineering to Architecture. Springer. 22 pp.

ecosystems have acquired distinctive features to adapt to their environments. Living things adapt to maintain vital activities such as feeding, sheltering, hunting, reproduction, and protection from their enemies. A similar situation applies to the relationship between accounting and technology. Accounting has changed and transformed to adapt to technological developments in the historical process. Accountants who use technology in accounting applications are the natural implementers of this evolutionary process. Technological innovations such as artificial intelligence and cloud technology systems are changing the functions of accounting and the competencies of accountants. In other words, they're transforming the accountants themselves.

Technological Evolution of Accounting

Accounting is an information system. When the amount of data included in this system increased, we began to utilize information technology. We used computer programs to store and record accounting data, and then MRP (material requirements planning) programs were added in manufacturing plants. During this process, ERP (enterprise resource planning) software was developed, and internet integration emerged over time. Today, machines and accounting programs can communicate instantly with each other over the 'internet of things'. Thanks to sensors placed on the machines, data obtained can be automatically transferred to the ERP program. This process rapidly progresses from static data to streamed data.[11]

While production data used to be collected manually on-site, today, data collection tools, such as sensors and actuators, are used to automatically collect data generated during production and business processes. This data reflects Industry 4.0 machine maintenance, product quality, environmental ecology, energy expenses, labor costs, locations of inventory, and so on. With smart production information

11 VASILEV, J. The change from ERP II to ERP III systems, Conference Paper July 2014 (3rd International Conference on Application of Information and Communication Technology and Statistics in Economy and Education (ICAICTSEE 2013), At Sofi)

systems, all processes are monitored instantly; data is collected from every point and transferred to the data processing center, creating a digital twin. The data can be accessed immediately, and deviations can be detected instantly with data analytics.

In the years ahead, accounting systems with self-learning capability will perform classical accounting operations such as calculation of sales, costs, liquidity, and invoice tracking. These systems will be protected with high security that will soon be made possible through artificial intelligence, blockchain technology, and the 4th Industrial Revolution. With digital transformation, accounting is evolving from paper data to digital documents, and from analysis to analytics.

In the technological evolution of accounting, new accounting practices always consist of improved combinations of old ones, and they themselves become potential components for the construction of more advanced applications in future. They are potential building blocks towards a more advanced accounting practice.

The technological evolutionary progress of the accounting profession means not only the sequencing of technical processes but also the determination of how this change mechanism works. Just as the previous technological development pioneered the new technological development, the previous accounting practices will also pioneer the new accounting applications. In short, the technological evolution of accounting is the theory of the transformation of accounting through technological development.

Digital Evolution of Accounting and Accountants

The transformation of accounting practices mainly depends on the state of technological knowledge. With applications such as e-book, e-invoice, and e-declaration, digitalization affects every step of the accounting profession from registration to declaration. Digital systems bring new materials and values for accountants to negotiate. Verbal culture leaves its place to digital and analytical culture. It is a digital evolution. So, what will the digital evolution of accounting be in the future? What will it look like?

Technology will constantly reshape the accounting profession. Cloud-based programs will become mainstream, and all professionals will have access to their clients' financial information at a single click of a button from wherever they are. This improvement, in turn, will affect office environments and the interactions between accountants and clients. Ways of doing business will increasingly shift to digital.

In this context, accounting is evolving into a multidisciplinary field that includes engineering methods, mathematical tools, and programming practices. With digital and technological developments, the profession is being transformed from A to Z in areas such as thinking, education, culture, and technology. This evolution directs professional accountants towards data analysis, strategy, and consultancy instead of classical records and statements. It is the result of the profession adapting to digitalization, and natural selection.

To summarize, the evolutionary cycles of accounting and accountants are affected by technological developments, and technological developments form their foundation. For the accounting profession to survive in the future, this evolution must be measurable, and accountants must manage their evolution.

According to the theory of evolution, the chances of survival for those who adhere to the traditional structure are very small. There is no possibility of the old structure being passed on to future generations. Darwin called this process the survival of the fittest and the adapted. One of the foundation stones of the evolutionary process is that all species adapt slowly but surely to changes in the world. When the historical development of accounting is examined in this context, we can see that accounting has evolved over the years and constantly adapted to changing technological conditions. Didn't manually recorded ledgers evolve into e-ledgers, and paper invoices into e-invoices? In the future, accounting practices that we don't yet know will emerge, and many applications used today will lose their validity.

In conclusion, the technological evolution of accounting offers a more holistic understanding of the profession's development by emphasizing the interaction between accounting and technology. The technological evolution approach to accounting can help us better understand and more easily prepare for the future digital transformation that will occur. In particular, it can serve as a guide and reference for redesigning accounting education. In this way, it can provide an opportunity to manage the technological changes and control their effects on professional practices and accounting systems.

CHAPTER II
THE FUTURE OF ACCOUNTING PROFESSION

Some people are futurists. They are defined by their focus on the future and modernity. These thinkers attempt to replace outmoded and traditional concepts with new ideas, creating a unique and dynamic vision for the future. Futurism was also the name of an avant-garde art movement that started in Italy in 1909, led by a charismatic poet named Filippo Tommaso Marinetti. The movement took speed as its inspiration, and technology and modernity as its starting point. Speed was essential to the dynamic character of twentieth-century life and was glorified in the age of machines.

In the 1950s, futurists predicted that robots and flying cars would become part of everyday life in the 2000s. Many of their predictions are coming true; just the timings weren't quite right! The world now stands on the brink of a technological revolution with the appearance of robot assistants, driverless vehicles, smart cities, wearable technology, space tourism, and even those flying cars. Many of these technologies will soon become mainstream and alter life significantly.

Mobile apps, from social media to Whatsapp, Uber and Netflix, have already changed our lives in just one decade. Some of today's biggest companies (think Airbnb, Tinder, Fitbit, Tumblr, Pinterest, and Indiegogo) were not yet in existence 15 years ago, while many of the things that were widely relied upon back then – corded phones, newspapers, desktop computers, camcorders, DVD and CD players – are now hardly used. Nowadays, technology rules our lives and is at the center of everything. It is very hard to imagine the world we live in today without smartphones, tablets, and laptops.[12]

According to a study conducted by research company Dscout, a person touches their phone 2,617 times a day, on average, and spends approximately five hours a day browsing the internet and using apps – equal to about a third of the time a person is awake.[13] Today, we

12 Frey, T., (2016) https://futuristspeaker.com/technology-trends/72-stunning-things-in-the-future-that-will-be-common-ten-years-from-now-that-dont-exist-today/

13 https://blog.dscout.com/mobile-touches

are building a digital infrastructure on almost every physical thing in the world. For humanity, the future is still uncertain and fascinating. The predictions listed below were made by technology experts and manufacturers participating in research by the world-renowned Pew Research Center. They are quite striking and, I believe, provide us with a vision for the future:[14]

1. **Technology forms the basis of everything in our life.**

Food, health, education, and work… We are moving towards a future of electric cars, flying personal machines, Hyperloop transport systems, space travel and asteroid mining. We will now attach band-type fitness sensors to our skin. Refrigerators will tell us when we run out of milk, we will charge our devices using wireless power, we will make sure that algorithms optimize and protect our homes. Some of these may or may not happen… However, one thing seems certain: technology will become smaller, smarter, and cheaper. In fact, everything will be so small that computers and sensors will fit almost anywhere.

2. **In the future, all technologies, large and small, will be sensory and responsive**.

Ubiquitous artificial intelligence systems will communicate with humans in the same way humans interact with each other. Sensors on our clothes, shoes and backpacks will measure the quality of the air we breathe. When we fill a glass with water, the sensors in the glass – before we drink – will measure the quality of the water. Our metabolism, body temperature, stress level and other health indicators will be measured continuously. Medical professionals will manufacture bespoke human organs and we will be living in an era of personalized healthcare.

3. **Autonomous vehicles will shape the future.**

Car manufacturers are turning towards producing cars without pedals or steering wheels. Every country in the world will be affected

---

14 https://www.pewresearch.org /

by the autonomous car industry and transportation will become faster, cheaper, and easier.

4. **In the future, we will be able to control our phones with the power of thought.**

Intervention in the human brain has long been a topic of interest. Can our brains be hacked to make them forget something or to erase uncomfortable feelings? Yes, why not? Technically, this would be possible if we had a microchip in our brains. Here is an even more puzzling question: if thoughts could be decoded, could they also be altered? What would happen if someone else could enter a person's brain and upload their own consciousness there?

For the first time ever, a team of South African biomedical engineers has succeeded in connecting a human brain to the internet in real time.[15] This is the first step towards brain controlled IoT applications. The "Brainternet" project transfers brain waves to the internet. The relevant technology may make it possible to perform bidirectional data transfer in the near future by sending electrical signals to the brain in the form of data. This technology could enable us to operate devices and machines by the power of thought in the future.

Elon Musk founded the company Neuralink in 2016 to develop brain-machine interfaces with remarkably high bandwidths. Musk's goal is to establish a direct connection between humans and computers through a chip placed in the human brain. He introduced the chip he plans to implant in July 2019.[16] With this chip, we will be able to connect our smart phones to our thoughts via Bluetooth and control them with thoughts. In the next phase, we will be able to load our brains with skills such as learning a foreign language or playing musical instruments.

When used for the benefit of humanity, technology eradicates

15 Gaughill, P., (2017), https://futurism.com/researchers-have-linked-a-human-brain-to-the-internet-for-the-first-time-ever

16 https://www.nytimes.com/2019/07/16/technology/neuralink-elon-musk.html

disease, it helps reduce hunger and extreme poverty, and it enables world-spanning flights and global communication. People now live longer, healthier lives, thanks to technology.

The world of the future will be an amazing place. Imagine your dreams being viewed on-screen by decoding the data in your brain. Now imagine your smartphone calling someone when it crosses your mind to call them. These are not just science fiction scenarios; they are on the way to becoming a part of our lives. As Marinetti, that pioneer of Futurism, said, "Let's give ourselves utterly to the Unknown, not in desperation but only to replenish the deep wells of the Absurd!"

II.1-INFORMATION SYSTEMS AND INFORMATION TECHNOLOGIES

We can talk about the similarity between information systems and information technologies, but these two concepts differ in many aspects. Information systems management is concerned with the solutions for tasks, and to what extent raw data can be managed and processed in systems to create new business opportunities. Information technology management, on the other hand, is the design and implementation of processes in which the information system can be used in the most effective and efficient way.

Information technologies cover all the equipment, processes, and people involved in the dissemination of information within an organization, and they represent computer network components that perform the processing and dissemination of business and personal information. The main difference between information systems and information technologies is that information systems focus on information. Even though technology facilitates the collection and processing of information, the primary issue is the information itself.

Information technologies are becoming more and more dependent on cloud systems with virtual machines. Soon, these cloud systems will evolve into smart computer networks, with additional functions. With no sign of slowing down in its development, information technology is a candidate for becoming the main determining factor among the forces that will shape our future. In this chapter, we will examine the nature of information technology, as well as its relentless pace, and we will see how it has already transformed the accounting profession.

Information Systems

Information systems are defined as a group of interrelated elements with the purpose of collecting, preserving, and disseminating information for planning, controlling, analysis, management, and decision-making purposes. To understand the structure of information systems, it is useful to first examine the concepts of "information" and "system".

Information is defined as all the phenomena, facts, and principles that can be comprehended by the human brain; it is truth obtained through learning, research, or observation, and is the intellectual product emerging as a result of the activity of the human mind. It can also be defined as the meaning that individuals refer to data by making use of rules. The word "information" derives from the Latin word *informare*, which means to shape the mind, to discipline and to teach.

System describes an order of processes used to achieve a result, way, or method, and consists of five basic components:

- **Input:** All elements entering the system for being processed.
- **Process:** All conversion actions that convert input to output.
- **Output:** Elements obtained at the end of the processing.
- **Feedback:** Data on the performance of the system.
- **Control:** Determining whether the system is working as intended by following the feedback.

When we examine these definitions, we see that the purpose of information systems is to provide support for planning, control, management, and decision processes by using the methods of collecting, processing, saving, transforming, and disseminating data and information.

Information system processes consist of recording, compilation, preparation, classification, separation, correction, tabulation, analysis, transformation, summarizing, sorting, and comparison activities.

The output of information systems is processed data and it can be obtained in various ways. For example, multimedia (combinations of formats such as audio, image, and video), paper products, audio responses, graphic images, forms, reports, and messages are all information system outputs. Feedback and control components are used for controlling the outputs. For example, a manager might discover that the final tally of sales quantities does not equal the total sales listed in the sales report. In this case, data and transactions can be checked again.

Information systems facilitate the management of externally provided information. The interrelated elements process the input received from the environment. They transform these inputs into outputs targeted by individuals or organizations. In other words, information systems transform information and data into meaningful outputs by subjecting them to various processes.

We can list the objectives of information systems as follows:

- To deliver reliable information on time, in appropriate formats, to where it is needed.
- To eliminate or minimize confusion about existing or potential situations within the organization.
- To provide information that managers can use in decision-making.
- To present important information enabling organizations to continue their activities effectively and to increase the quality of produced goods and services.

Information systems can be classed in many ways. Business activities and the system's role in management are often taken into account when determining their classification. In this respect, information systems are divided into **operation support systems** and **management support systems**. These systems can be detailed as follows:

A) Operation support systems: These are run to process data generated from or used in business activities. They are divided into three groups:

- *Activity processing systems*
- *Process control systems*
- *Corporate collaboration systems*

B) Management support systems: These provide information and help managers to make correct and effective decisions. They are examined in three groups:

- *Management information systems*
- *Decision support systems*
- *Executive information systems*

As information technology continues to advance, it embraces companies and the entire economy more powerfully. In this era, businesses are able to manage all their processes, including accounting, through the support they receive from information systems. The use of information systems in accounting and financial reporting processes directly affects the review, storage, and transmission of financial data and changes the structure of the internal control environment.

In 2002, telecommunications company WorldCom was embroiled in one of the largest US accounting scandals after internal auditors used the company's information systems to uncover a $4 billion fraudulent expense allocation (among other fraudulent accounting inputs).[17] Information systems also played an important role in investigating the 2008 collapse of Lehman Brothers – the world's largest bankruptcy in history. The failure of this giant investment bank, whose roots dated back to 1844, was described as the biggest economic crisis after the Great Depression in 1929, and even US federal reserve president Alan Greenspan described it as the "crisis of the century".

As can be seen from these examples, developments in information systems directly affect the scope and development of accounting.

Accounting Information Systems

The accounting information system is a sub-system of the management information system and comprises both "financial accounting information" and "management accounting information".

The purpose of the financial accounting information system is to

17 WorldCom (Firm). Board of Directors. Special Investigative Committee, Beresford, D. R., Katzenbach, N. D., & Rogers, C. B. (2003). *Report of investigation*. Findlaw.

provide internal information flow within the business. It presents the activities carried out by the business and includes its debts and assets.

Management accounting information, on the other hand, is the interpretation of accounting information for the purpose of managing the activities of the business. Business owners and managers use this information (in addition to non-accounting information) in determining the objectives of the business, evaluating the performance of employees, planning, and executing activities, and making management decisions.

As a whole, the accounting information system focuses on the activities carried out within the company and the data flow resulting from these activities. It has two main objectives. The first is to protect the assets of the enterprise and to determine the changes that occur in these assets over time. The second is to provide information to third parties regarding the financial status of the enterprise and the results of its activities.

This latter communication stage ensures that accounting information helps third parties outside the business make decisions. A business may have exceptionally good accounting records but if they are not properly communicated to third parties, the intended purpose of accounting will not be achieved, and the accounting system will become meaningless.

The relationship that information users have with the business is important in determining what kind of information will be provided, and who gets to see what. In other words, determining user groups helps establish the intended use of accounting information and indicates what kind of information should be disclosed to whom and in what ways. The accounting information system directly affects financial and non-financial processes. It also paves the way for the integration of accounting with technology, other information, and managerial approaches.

A well-designed accounting information system ensures that a business runs problem-free on a daily basis. When a business is in trouble, however, the data present in the accounting information system is an important argument in the story of what has gone wrong.

According to the Greek philosopher Heraclitus, “the only unchanging thing in the universe is change itself”. Of course, the disruptive technologies of our age also affect accounting information systems, which are being reshaped in parallel with fintech (financial technology), the new product of the digital world. Practices similar to using mobile devices and applications are used in accounting (albeit in a limited way for the time being), especially in the finance and banking sector. Further changes in accounting technologies will only continue to increase the rate of change in accounting and accounting information systems.

So, how will academics, accounting institutions and professional accountants make use of technology to transform the accounting profession for the better? Are they ready for it?

II.2-INFORMATION TECHNOLOGIES

Information technology can be defined as a combination of computer and communication technology. It includes all technologies related to data collection, processing, and delivery.

In enterprise settings, these technologies are relied on for guidance in decision-making. They do this by providing information when needed, within the decision-making mechanisms of the organization. In other words, information technologies are those technologies that allow effective and efficient operations by recording data, processing it, accessing the information produced, storing it, and then transmitting the information required.

Information technologies necessitate a set of constantly changing skills and structures that require creativity to maintain. They enable businesses to make accurate predictions about the future and provide them with the opportunity to make rational decisions and to communicate effectively with parties inside and outside the organization.

With the development of information technologies, we are now able to manage business relations with colleagues and customers thousands of kilometers away, within flexible working hours, using mobile telephones, video conferencing, email, and instant messaging.

Historical Process of Information Technology

The first instrument that comes to mind when thinking of early information technology is a machine developed by French inventor Blaise Pascal in the seventeenth century. It was a device that could perform two operations: addition and subtraction. A commercial calculating model was soon developed that could perform four operations. The Industrial Revolution increased mechanization and invented new production techniques. One discovery was that punch cards could be used to automate weaving looms. Such developments allowed people to do their jobs more practically and quickly.

Even though the abacus, used since the Babylonian Empire in the 2400s BCE, is regarded as an ancestor of computers, the first analog computer didn't come into being until American inventor Vannevar Bush built it in 1931. Howard H. Aiken then made an automatic computer for IBM in 1939 using semi-electronic circuits, which he called Mark I. This computer worked as an advanced calculator and weighed five tons.

Computers were developed further for military purposes during World War II and contributed to decisions made in the military field. In 1941, the first programmable electronic computer named ENIAC was invented. These room-sized computers began to get smaller and faster after the invention of transistors in 1947.

Briton Alan Turing was one of the greatest mathematicians of the twentieth century and is considered the inventor of computer science and artificial intelligence. Together with Gordon Welchman, he developed an electro-mechanical device named "Bombe" during World War II that deciphered the codes of Enigma, Nazi Germany's code encryption machine. Historians estimate that breaking the Enigma codes shortened the war by more than two years, saving 14 million lives.

In the second half of the twentieth century, information technology began to be used increasingly in developed countries in the fields of agriculture, industry, and service, as well as in education, health, and communication. The most important benefit was the increase in production and efficiency, but information technology also brought economic, technological, social, and cultural developments along with it. Other countries were soon affected as well: information technology enabled countries to get closer to each other in economic, political, social, and cultural terms.

In the twenty-first century, information technology has reached such a stage that many people in China have stopped using paper money altogether and instead pay for most transactions with applications such as "WeChat Pay". In the USA and UK, the world's largest online shopping platform Amazon has launched cashier-free physical stores through the app Amazon Go, which allows customers to shop cash-free by automatically scanning barcodes as they put items in their baskets. Meanwhile, "augmented reality" has become a part of education. Language learning app Mondly has recently launched an AR-based virtual teacher system to help users practice their skills – practicing as if they were interacting with people in real life.

Today, about two billion people do not leave their homes without a smartphone, and they can buy almost any product imaginable on the internet. Whether we admit it or not, we are all dependent on technology and it's hard to imagine life without it. These developments will fundamentally reshape the way we work, both as companies and individuals.

Evolving technology tirelessly analyzes our data, delivers actionable insights, and correlates our financial data with external data to provide new context. Speed is the hallmark of information technology, and accounting benefits considerably. Businesses can access and transfer financial information much more quickly and much more accurately. They can keep their accounting information in a database that they can access from anywhere at any time. The time required by accountants to prepare and present financial information to management is significantly shortened, and company executives can create individual reports quickly and easily, helping them to make decisions. In the twenty-first century, having rapid access to the right information is fundamental to strategic superiority.

Undoubtedly, information technology has always had, and will continue to have, a profound impact on the accounting profession, and it is vital that accountants follow new IT developments. New technologies are forcing accountants to acquire new tools and skills and take their practices to a much higher level. It is no longer possible to make do with Excel knowledge. In future, all information technologies in the accounting field will become smart technologies. Accounting programs that are able to recognize a specific transactor, communicate, perceive what is happening around them, enable accounting records through voice commands, and independently present accounting reports, such as balance sheets and income statements, will probably emerge. What will an accountant reading this in 100 years' time think of these predictions, I wonder?

II.3-PROFESSIONS AND TECHNOLOGY

People in industry are frequently replaced by automation systems in the workforce rationalization process. Armies of typesetting and analog printing workers were pushed aside by new printing technologies. Who now remembers typing pools? Wasn't a bank clerk once synonymous with secure employment? Are the days of German car manufacturers having more people than robots on the automotive assembly lines long gone? Many of these changes in work organization have gone relatively unnoticed.

Technology-induced unemployment and changes in production technologies are at the top of the agenda for global industry. According to a survey participated in by more than 500 C-suite executives in Europe and the USA, nearly 40 percent of Fortune 500 companies are expected to disappear by 2025 due to megatrends such as digitalization.[18] The same fears were at the forefront of people's minds with the mechanization of the Industrial Revolution in England 200 years ago. Eventually, businesses and professions will have to reinvent themselves in the digital age.

Technological advancements have been continually reshaping professions since the First Industrial Revolution. However, the speed of automation is such that it can fundamentally change the dynamics of the business world, and today's pace is unprecedented. Today, we are in an age where fashion companies turn into fashion houses, newspapers into membership clubs, electricity companies into software companies, and car manufacturers into transportation networks; almost all business lines are changing.

Researchers Carl Benedikt Frey and Michael A. Osborn from Oxford University examined possible professions that could be taken over by computer algorithms in 20 years' time in their 2013 study

18 Muller, H., (2020) Future State 2025: How Top Technology Executives Disrupt and Drive Success in the Digital Economy

"The Future of Employment".[19] According to the study, 47 percent of occupations in the USA are at high risk. For example, there is a 99 percent probability that algorithms will have taken over telemarketing and insurance work by 2033. Some 98 percent of referees, 97 percent of cashiers, 96 percent of chefs, 94 percent of both waiters and lawyer assistants, and 91 percent of tour guides are expected to lose their jobs. New technologies will transform much of what we know about the way people work.

Perhaps in the future, there will be robots in all aspects of daily life. Apple's Siri and IBM's Watson are the first steps towards fully personalized digital assistants. Future generations of such products will open the door to all sorts of new social interactions and situations that affect human relationships in ways we cannot yet imagine. The jobs of the future will be done by humans and machines in collaboration.

A digital culture urges people to produce results faster, and having a digital culture is an important criterion for attracting digital talent. However, when it comes to digital transformation, people often ignore the importance of having a digital culture already in place. It is important because transformation is an ongoing process. You need to create a culture that values change before you can become digital. Culture leads the adoption of technology, and our ability to innovate depends on the impatience of that culture.

The new business language of the accounting industry is digitalization and technology. The American Institute of Certified Public Accountants (AICPA) cites "information technology application skills" as having moved to the top of the knowledge and skills requirements for entry-level accounting. Accounting education has also been affected by technological developments. American and European universities have opened new accounting technology departments to prepare students to adapt and deal with increasingly complex digital accounting practices.

---

19 Frey, C. B., & Osborne, M. A. (2013). The future of employment: how susceptible are jobs to computerization? (2013). Oxford: Oxford Martin Programme on the Impacts of Future Technology

In the last decade, many digital systems have entered our lives within the scope of tax services, and it is not possible for accountants to be unaffected. This new structuring urges all professions and professional organizations to seek new-approach models. According to McKinsey, the US management consultancy, 86 percent of accounting tasks are already automated with existing technology.[20] In addition, the global stay-at-home measures during the Covid-19 pandemic have accelerated a trend for working in virtual offices and communicating via video conferencing.

20 https://www.mckinsey.com/business-functions/mckinsey-digital/our-insights/where-machines-could-replace-humans-and-where-they-cant-yet

Table 2. Susceptibility of professions to computerization

Recreational Therapists	0,28%
Doctors and Surgeons	0,42%
Career and Technical Education Teachers, Middle Schools	0,88%
Sales Managers	1,30%
Chief Executives	1,50%
Authors	3,80%
Nuclear Engineers	7,00%
Police Officers (on patrol duty)	9,80%
Cabin Attendants/ Flight Personnel	35,00%
Economists	43,00%
Police Officers, Fire Fighters, Ambulance Dispatchers	49,00%
Commercial Pilots	55,00%
Librarians	65,00%
Medical Secretaries	81,00%
Executive Secretaries and Assistants	86,00%
Taxi Drivers and Private Chauffeurs	89,00%
Accountants and Auditors	94,00%
Cashiers	97,00%
Bookkeeping, Accounting, and Audit Personnel	98,00%
Tax Preparers	99,00%

Source: *Turmob XX: Accounting Congress Presentation by Prof. Dr. Melih Erdogan 2018.*

As you can see from the table, accounting is one of the professions most likely to be affected by computerization and technological developments. Digital transformation offers us smart accounting applications, and as solutions for simplified automation continue to come, the need for manual data entry is increasingly eliminated, reducing the likelihood of mistakes. However, even as technology opens up new opportunities and new career fields for accountants, it also harbors the danger of extinction for the profession. For accounting to be more effective in the future, it needs to operate under a new model of practice that can respond to the digitalization and e-transformation process. This modeling should prepare the accounting profession for the future by rebuilding it from A to Z in areas such as thinking, education, culture, and technology. Let us take a brief look at these technologies now.

II.4-NEW TECHNOLOGIES AND THEIR IMPACT ON ACCOUNTING

Digital transformation is just part of a larger organizational structure, but it is now the main factor affecting the future of all fields of activity. Innovation therefore has to be about much more than developing new technologies reactively. Cultivating a culture that encourages change and innovation is crucial. Using technology to transform the accounting profession begins with belief and mindset.

Although "the human touch" is still a valuable tool for accountants, there is no way to escape new technology (at least not for those who hope to remain employable). It is quite difficult to beat the speed, efficiency, and accuracy of new technologies, and accountants who can integrate them into their accounting processes will undoubtedly be considered more valuable in the future.

Technological developments that will shape the future of accounting include accounting software, artificial intelligence, robotic technology (RPA), cloud systems, Industry 4.0, blockchain technology, radio frequency identification technology, big data, 3D printing technologies, internet of things (IoT), augmented reality, Society 5.0, and cyber security technologies. There is no doubt that technologies will become more flexible and powerful in the coming years, but what will they mean for the accounting profession? How can the accounting profession benefit from their strength?

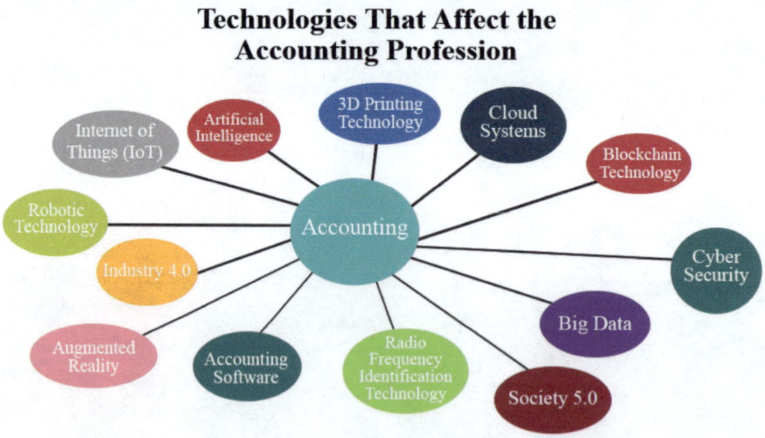

Figure 1. Technologies that affect the accounting profession

Accounting Software Programs

Accounting software programs record and process accounting operations within the functional modules of a business and allow easy preparation of financial reports. In short, all accounting functions, such as determining, classifying, summarizing, and reporting accounting operations and events, can now be carried out with computer programs. Many operations can be done more reliably and more quickly than using traditional methods. Accounting programs can be grouped under three headings:

- **General Accounting Programs:** These allow the monitoring of accounting transactions in a computer environment and transform invoices and similar documents showing business activities prepared in different environments into accounting receipts. These programs, which basically enable businesses to make declarations and notifications to government agencies more quickly, are still used by various businesses and accounting offices to record incomes and expenses, and to keep track of cash entries and exits as well as the balances of customers and suppliers. The biggest shortcoming of this type of system is that it does not produce much information that businesses can use in decision-making.
- **Semi-Automatic Integrated Systems:** This type of system carries out more business activities and transactions in a computer environment than in general accounting package programs. They generally consist of sub-modules, such as orders, delivery slips, invoices, current, check-promissory notes, accounting, stock, production, inventory, operating ledger, personnel, and budgets. The modules can operate independently, or they can be integrated with each other. Some of the activities included in the declarations and notifications to be submitted to state institutions, which must be entered in the general accounting environment, are also within this scope. Recording these activities as accounting slips, and processing them within the scope of accounting, are also among the functions of semi-automatic systems. They tend to be used in small and medium-sized businesses, and in both developing and established accounting offices.

- **Fully Automatic Integrated Systems:** These systems allow all the activities performed in semi-automatic integrated systems to be automatically converted into accounting slips. In terms of operations, these systems are more advanced than the first two types. They require financial resources and qualified personnel and are mostly used in medium and large-scale enterprises that can meet these requirements. The best example of fully automatic integrated systems is enterprise resource planning (ERP) systems. These are software programs that integrate different departments of an organization into the same system. These different departments (manufacturing, finance, sales, etc.) enter accounting-related records and information, and this is sent to the accounting department for interpretation and analysis. From this, a report on the status and future of the company can be created. ERP systems, which access information rapidly, safely, and easily, have made a significant contribution to the profession's ability to keep up with the modern age.

A significant number of large enterprises use ERP systems such as SAP and Oracle, which provide accounting support among other business functions. ERP systems are currently the most effective information technologies used in accounting, which is why employers demand that accountants be competent in using them.

Artificial Intelligence

Intelligence is defined in humans as having the ability to think, reason, perceive objective facts, judge, and draw conclusions. Human features and qualities such as understanding, evaluation, planning, and problem solving are evaluated within this scope. Artificial intelligence can be defined as the ability of computers or robots to perform actions with qualities peculiar to living things. In other words, artificial intelligence means creating an ideal copy of living intelligence.

In 1950, British codebreaker Alan Turing, who had made it possible for certain complex mathematical calculations to be performed by mechanism, posed the question: "Can machines think?" In pursuit of an answer, he invented the Turing test, and became a pioneer of modern computer science.[21] In the 1930s, he and fellow scientist Kurt Godel had conducted research in the field of mathematics and logic and claimed that systematic algorithms that produce all of the solutions in certain mathematical clusters were not possible. However, the human mind, applied organically, seems capable of solving all of the problems in at least some of these clusters.

More recently, American computer scientist John McCarthy defined the phenomenon of intelligence as the computational part of human competence that is required to achieve our goals on Earth; he saw artificial intelligence as the science of transferring the intelligence seen in humans and animals to computers through computer programs.

AI researchers argue that if artificial intelligence can make the transition to general intelligence, then there will be no reason for machines not to achieve full human intelligence. A lot of work is being done today to teach emotion to machines, but smart machines may never be able to fully replace the benefits of human emotion and intuition, and I think there will always be a difference between artificial and human intelligence for this reason.

Artificial intelligence is, however, an effective, fast, and inexpensive tool that is helping to steer the twenty-first century. Microsoft co-founder Bill Gates considers the rise of AI the "Holy Grail" of computer science. We can foresee a future where, with the development of artificial intelligence, people will no longer have to drive cars or go to a doctor to diagnose their diseases. We are entering a new technological era where human beings will no longer need to be involved at every stage of business, from production to marketing, because robots can carry out the commands. Thus, it seems that unemployment could be a serious problem in countries that have become global production bases.

The AI accounting program SMACC, developed jointly by Cherry Ventures, Rocket Internet, Dieter von Holtzbrinck Ventures and

---

21 Warwick, K., & Shah, H. (2016). Can machines think? A report on Turing test experiments at the Royal Society. *Journal of experimental & Theoretical artificial Intelligence*, *28*(6), 989-1007.

Grazia Equity, automatically reads company invoices and documents into a system protected with high security, and records them in accounting accounts without external intervention. The system, which can perform operations such as sales and cost calculation, invoice tracking, and liquidity calculation, also has the capability to learn by itself.[22] For example, the system checks the items in the invoices, total amounts, and tax rates, it verifies the results and, once it learns the special rates used for certain products or suppliers, applies them in subsequent transactions. SMACC is not the only program made with artificial intelligence, and the use of such programs will only become more common over time. AI and machine learning will become part of the future of accounting.

Cognitive computing uses artificial intelligence and machine-learning algorithms to go beyond analytical capabilities in order to make autonomous decisions, to learn, and to cause – at an increasing rate – profound structural changes in industries. Intelligent systems will increasingly take over the decision-making process from humans. We need to understand the impact of artificial intelligence on the business world and how accountants can participate in the process. Accountants have been actively using technology for many years to add more value to businesses, and AI could be a new opportunity to reassess and radically improve the quality of business and investment decisions – which is the ultimate goal of our profession.

Should accountants be alarmed by the advancement of artificial intelligence? We still need human intuition and emotions. If we understand the practical difficulties of AI systems and the required skills, we can work together in harmony, increasing the efficiency and effectiveness of accounting. Artificial intelligence will analyze and interpret data, but accountants will still be needed, especially those who can provide consultancy services. To create a vision for the future, we need to know how AI can solve accounting problems, what it means for the future of accounting, and which skills accountants will need to work with smart systems.

---

22 Ozdogan, B. (2017). The future of the accounting profession in an era of start-ups. *Accounting and corporate reporting-today and tomorrow.*

When artificial intelligence applications turn into real consultants that can offer opinions, more accounting errors and costs will be prevented. That is to say, if AI accounting programs are programmed to fully comply with the laws in tax legislation, they will comply with this command exactly. Likewise, if they are programmed to notify you when they detect an illegal document, they will do that, too.

The effects of artificial intelligence on the accounting profession can be placed under three headings:

- Can artificial intelligence solve accounting problems?

  AI technology can correct errors and solve problems that occur during manual data entries. For example, it can detect and correct differences that may occur between bank accounts and accounting records. It can determine payments made for more than one invoice and match them with the relevant individual invoices. It can find a combination of equal numbers and it can detect in a very short time the paid and unpaid invoices of a firm that issues thousands of invoices every month.

  As a result, artificial intelligence is at a level where it can perform manual accounting operations such as reconciliation transactions and solve problems that occur.

- Will artificial intelligence eliminate the accounting profession?

  Even though accounting programs provide convenience, most of the work is still done by accountants. AI accounting programs will eliminate classical processes such as data entry, notifications, and declarations, but it will not completely eliminate the accounting profession or accountants; it will only reduce the need for them. As a result, many professional accountants will turn their focus to other tasks, such as consultancy, and will need new skills, such as data strategy, statistical analysis, probability, and deduction and reasoning.

- Are statements and notifications made by artificial intelligence legally valid?

  When systems and robots with artificial intelligence act as members of the accounting profession, who will have legal and criminal responsibility for their work and actions? Who will be responsible for the statements and notifications made by AI systems? Is it the manufacturers of these systems, their users, or the entity itself? There is no legal regulation on AI systems yet, but it will be needed in the coming years.

If artificial intelligence and robots are considered within their legal dimensions, the first issue that needs to be examined is existential status. On the one hand, the robot has no manager or controller; it can make its own decisions. Therefore, if it acts consciously of its own "will" and causes an error to occur in the declaration and accounting processes, it must be responsible for that error.

On the other hand, there is an argument, voiced by Turkish IT lawyer Atty. Unsal Ozmestik at a meeting of the Istanbul Bar Association Informatics Commission, for comparing the legal nature of AI systems to the legal nature of slaves in Roman Law. He explained: "The slaves … were considered goods in Roman Law and [their] owners were responsible for their actions because they did not have rights and legal capacity".

This issue will need to be resolved by lawyers in the near future.

Robotic Technology – Robotic Process Automation (RPA)

Robotic Process Automation is a software that performs business process activities in a faster, more accurate, and more convenient manner. Leslie Willcocks, a professor at the London School of Economics, defines it as "the type of software that mimics a person's act of performing a task in the process".[23] RPA automates and accelerates repetitive tasks and routine operations; its greatest advantage over humans is its speed and accuracy. It can also work externally, connected to ERP systems.

The Chinese company Changying Precision Technology has achieved a 250 percent increase in productivity by changing 90

23 Willcocks, L., Lacity, M., & Craig, A. (2017). Robotic process automation: strategic transformation lever for global business services? *Journal of Information Technology Teaching Cases*, *7*(1), 17-28.

percent of its manpower-based business model to a model based on robots.[24] Bill Gates has even made a call for robots replacing human workers to be required to pay taxes.

While RPA constantly improves the work it does, it does not incur additional costs as the human-oriented workforce does, and it works on a 24/7 basis.

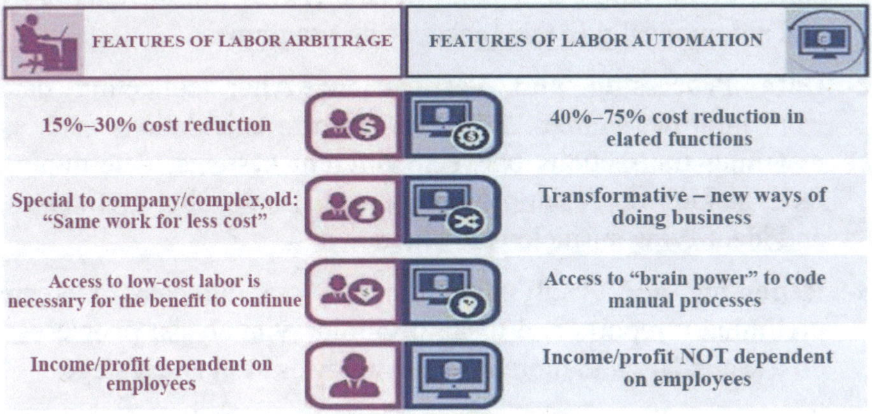

Figure 2. Labor Arbitrage – Labor Automation[25]

With RPA, hundreds of millions of call center and information workers across the world are at risk of losing their jobs.[26] It does, however, provide a solution for countries with aging populations.

Robotic processes that have taken place in the manufacturing, transportation, and medical industries perform accounting and finance tasks previously undertaken by humans, including invoice equalization, variance analysis and reconciliations. By using RPA, accountants no longer need to carry out recording and manual operations, nor struggle with reconciling thousands of instances

---

24 Forrest, C. (2015). Chinese factory replaces 90% of humans with robots, production soars. *Tech Republic*.

25 Kaynak: /home.kpmg.com/tr/tr/home/gorusler/2016/09/dijital-isgucu-geliyor-yaklasan-dijital-isgucu-dalgasi.html

26 Fingar, C. T. (Ed.). (2009). *Global trends 2025: A transformed world.* DIANE Publishing.

of data. RPA simplifies processes while increasing efficiency and enabling end-to-end automation.

Accounting tasks that robot automation processes can perform include:

1- **Data Import:** RPAs can record the accounting records of bank cards, credit cards, and point-of-sale (POS) transactions daily and automatically in their accounting programs.

2- **Data Processing and Verification:** After collecting data from multiple sources, RPA can perform calculations such as matching transactions between different systems, determining fees, making depreciation arrangements, balancing certificates, and identifying suspicious fluctuations.

3- **Reporting and Analysis:** RPAs can use the data to create preliminary reports and make preliminary analysis; people can do a secondary and more in-depth analysis at the next stage.

4- **Auditing:** Since RPAs can perform most of the manual and routine operations, accountants can focus on performing integrity, accuracy, and auditing functions rather than seeking and correcting human errors.

5- **Detecting Inconsistencies:** RPAs can detect inconsistencies in the records. Even if the RPA cannot resolve inconsistencies, it can forward them to an accountant for investigation.

The Cloud System

Cloud technology is the generic name for web-based information services that can be used and shared on computers and smart devices at any time, without requiring installation. Cloud technology has made download and storage operations easier and more reliable. Moving the most advanced artificial intelligence systems to clouds will certainly speed up white-collar automation. Today, cloud technologies are becoming a major competitive arena among technology leaders, such as Amazon, Google, and Microsoft.

A computer or smart device with internet access is needed to use a cloud system. Cloud systems operate on a user-server basis over web protocols. Users access these applications, and output appears on the server side. For example, when the user wants to run a word processor, the cloud system determines a suitable application and makes this visible in the web browser on the user's system, while also reserving local memory space for it on there. The server records all performed operations. It is a system that produces a total result, from creating files to modifying them.

In the field of accounting, cloud systems allow users to access programs such as CRM and ERP, as well as finance and accounting software, over the internet. Accounting systems are changing with cloud computing services, and a new business model is emerging with cloud accounting software.

Benefits of the Cloud System

Before cloud computing was invented, data was stored on hard or fixed disks. These limited storage areas could be inadequate when the amount of data was large. Cloud technology not only provided the opportunity to physically get rid of hard disks, but also brought advantages such as more storage space, fast data transfer, and cost savings. The cloud system has eliminated a very substantial workload in large companies.

According to a global survey by the World Economic Forum in 2020, 44 percent of human resource decision makers named new technologies as the main driver of increased remote working and teleconferencing.[27] Advances in mobile and cloud technology that simultaneously allow remote and instant access were selected as the most significant technological driving force to enable the rapid deployment of internet-based service models.

Cloud-based systems not only help staff work more efficiently from home, but they also allow many people to work on files at the same time, encouraging collaboration. This approach provides transparency, which helps teams better manage their workloads. Cloud-based systems are not only about working remotely, however;

---

27 http://www3.weforum.org/docs/WEF_Future_of_Jobs_2020.pdf

they also allow finance teams to focus on more value-added tasks, such as presenting business strategies, and evaluating and integrating performance management.

Risks of the Cloud System

In addition to all the benefits of the cloud system, there are also some risks:

- **Data Security and User Privacy:** In the cloud system, data is at risk because the security of user data is provided by a server in a different geographic location. This may result in companies' confidential information falling into the wrong hands.
- **Continuity of Service:** The server may authorize an external service to manage and process data operations. When services are not running, it can be difficult for users to access their data. Since the system is huge and open to everyone, a harmful structure can have negative consequences. However, when your internet access is very fast, even if there are interruptions elsewhere, you can continue your business, thanks to parallel use.
- **Data Problems When Changing Cloud Provider:** A possible service provider failure may cause problems for users.

Despite the risks, these systems have significant advantages. One is the job opportunities it creates. According to research by Microsoft and International Data Corporation (IDC), cloud computing will have created more than 130,000 job opportunities in Turkey alone between 2017 and 2022 and will cause the emergence of four new professions there: cloud computing expertise, large data analysis, shared vehicle driving and driverless vehicle engineering. These new job opportunities also affect the IT sector, and the fields of marketing, sales, finance, management, production, and service.

Cloud accounting

Cloud accounting applications run on remote servers and are accessed via a web browser. The most important advantage of cloud systems for the accounting profession is that they allow full access to real-time data, which means account balances are always correct. Cloud accounting also requires less maintenance than its traditional counterpart, with the cloud provider performing backups and automatic updates. Dependency on paperwork is significantly reduced. The Covid-19 outbreak forced many accountants to adapt to new working methods, and those who had cloud-based accounting software immediately had a significant advantage.

There are a few fundamental differences between cloud accounting programs and traditional accounting programs. First, cloud accounting programs are more flexible. Accounting data can be accessed from any device with an internet connection instead of just from several computers located in the company offices. Second, cloud accounting software automatically updates financial information and financial reports which can be accessed in real time. This real-time overview is crucial for businesses examining their cash position, planning future spending, or making major financial and strategic decisions.

The differences between classical accounting programs and cloud computing-based accounting programs can be seen in the following table:

Table 3. Comparative analysis of accounting programs and cloud computing-based accounting programs[28]

Conventional Accounting Programs	Cloud Computing-Based Accounting Programs
Remote access to the system is difficult.	Remote access to the system is possible.
Installation and updates are done manually.	Installation and updates are made automatically.
Limited opportunity to work independently outside the workplace.	Opportunity to work independently outside the workplace.
Backups are made at the local terminal.	Backups can be made both in the cloud computing system and at the local terminal.
Legislative changes are followed up individually.	Legislative changes are tracked through the cloud information system.
Frequent time loss in operations.	No time loss in transactions.
Invoices and other official documents are filled in and sent manually.	Invoices and other official documents are filled in and sent via the internet.
Business managers cannot access financial data remotely whenever they want.	Business managers can access financial data remotely whenever they want.
Accountants are not in constant contact with their client businesses.	Accountants are in constant contact with client businesses via web-based communications.

28 https://www.dia.com.tr/bulut-bilisim-muhasebe/?cv=1,

Businesses using cloud computing-based accounting systems can purchase as many computing, storage, and connectivity resources as they need and manage them over the media themselves. The virtual structure allows businesses to make cost savings on investment, renovation, infrastructure, management, etc, and their increasing service demands can be met much more flexibly and quickly. Companies such as Microsoft, Google and Amazon are investing billions of dollars in cloud computing, and almost every hi-tech company is working to develop a new cloud service.

The Covid-19 pandemic shed light on the importance of accurate and up-to-date financial information and digital sharing. In this period especially, businesses that operated their accounting systems via the cloud system were able to maintain uninterrupted connections with banks. In this way they were able to access implementation processes in a simpler and faster way than those using desktop-based software or those not using any software at all.

Fourth Industrial Revolution (Industry 4.0)

The first mechanical systems utilizing the power of water were invented with the First Industrial Revolution, which occurred towards the end of the eighteenth century. In these years, steam power began to be used more and various machines were produced. With the Second Industrial Revolution in the twentieth century, electrical energy was put into use and mass production began. The first electric production line came with this revolution. In the 1970s, with the automation of production processes, combined with electronic and information technologies, the Third Industrial Revolution began. This is when programmable smart control devices were invented.

The ongoing Fourth Industrial Revolution, first cited in Hannover in Germany in 2011 and also known as Industry 4.0, has enabled the integration of information and internet processes into production phases, as well as the creation of inter-process networks. The German federal government has provided significant support for this revolution. Industry 4.0 is about smart industry, smart factories, and smart production.

Many innovations are being developed in this period, such as: transferring production phases to robots, the development of artificial intelligence, the ability to produce items at home using three-dimensional printers, nanotechnology, and analysis and evaluation of big data. These all, in turn, lead to further economic and social transformation.

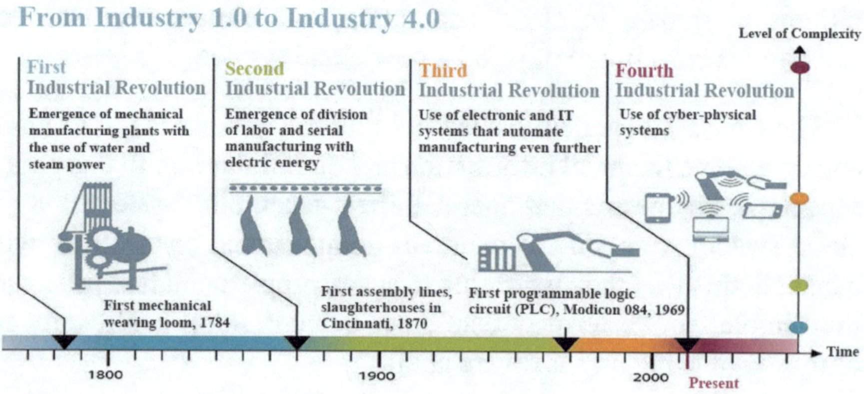

Figure 3. Historical development of industry[29]

While only large manufacturers and companies with a significant budget used to use cloud analytics, such as sensors, now businesses of all sizes can take advantage of these tools to speed up production. Industry 4.0 also aids production with time and inventory management tools, ensuring organizations have control of the end-to-end value chain throughout a product's life cycle. Thus, it is now possible to meet the customization demands of customers.

In this Fourth Industrial Revolution, it can be predicted that remote machines, each driven by different computers, will come under the networked control of main computers as a whole. Statistics and algorithms are becoming essential information and essential decision-making tools.

In the near future, smart machines that can communicate with each

29 http://www.capital.com.tr/images

other will have an important place in industry. These smart machines will adjust production, find system errors, and constantly monitor the conditions of physical objects and production activities to make real-time decisions. When they detect a malfunction, they will be able to immediately intervene and divert production to other machines. In the long run, factories will have the ability to adapt in real time to changes in market demand, technology options and regulation. There are smart factories that are already doing this today. Smart factories are at the heart of Industry 4.0, and machines are starting to develop strategies for creative solutions.

As smart factories collect and integrate accounting and other auditing information along the entire value chain, it becomes easier for accountants and auditors to monitor, control, and analyze the accounting data flows in the organization. Conducting audits and achieving real-time assurance increases the quality of auditing and accounting. Auditors can analyze larger volumes of data from a variety of sources to provide definitive assurance. With Industry 4.0, accountants will move away from bookkeeping and tax services and become strategic partners for businesses. Accountants will both gain and add value in the Fourth Industrial Revolution.

Industry 4.0 is a challenge for the accounting profession, but it also offers an opportunity for those who embrace it. The potential implications for the profession are listed below:

- A new accounting era may emerge, based on digital connectivity and common data platforms that facilitate real-time data exchange and problem solving.
- Data that cannot be obtained by professional accountants in real time will begin to be obtained via robotic systems.
- Quality, accuracy, and efficiency levels in accounting data will increase.
- Self-controlling and self-auditing accounting systems can emerge with smart factories.
- Decision-making processes will accelerate further as access to data in large common pools becomes easier.

In the Fourth Industrial Revolution, accountants will have less control over more accounting data. In the coming years, many operations currently done by accountants will be carried out by automation systems. So, will accountants find themselves redundant? If the profession restructures in line with the changes in the digital field, and if visionary ideas and models that can adapt to the digitalization process are produced, I think it will survive.

Blockchain Technology

Soon after the US financial crisis in 2008, an anonymous person (or persons) who called themselves Satoshi Nakamoto launched the digital currency system Bitcoin. This cryptocurrency, which relies on blockchain technology, allows people to make transactions securely without the need for third parties or a centralized structure, and thus raises questions about the future of the digital money and banking industry. For the first time in history, in fact, we can transfer money across national borders without being dependent on any central structure, in a cheaper, easier, and faster way than any conventional method practiced before.

Blockchain is a decentralized distributed digital ledger technology. It is a distributed database that provides tracking with encrypted transactions. Its greatest convenience is that every user can connect to the network, make new transactions, and verify transactions without any intermediaries. The information entered in the blockchain cannot be deleted, everyone can see the content of the record, and the records can only be updated if the relevant parties all mutually agree on it. It is these features that make the use of blockchain superior to other systems.

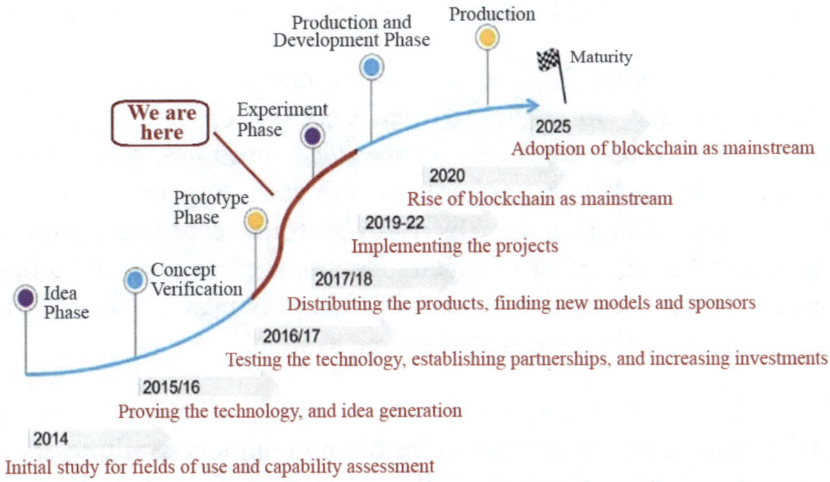

Figure 4. Historical development of blockchain technology and its future[30]

Analysts around the world view blockchain technology as an important part of the future for many organizations. In theory, the absence of a central authority is what makes blockchain fast. In fact, blockchain is more advantageous than many technologies not only in terms of processes that need speed in a decentralized technology environment, but also in terms of trust, transparency, and cost. It also creates higher independence than paper-based legacy storage systems, and it eliminates reconciliations.

Blockchain has the potential to particularly benefit the accounting profession as it reduces the traditional transaction costs of accounting and provides certainty on the ownership and history of assets. It also enables users to access ledgers in real time, as well as create smart contracts and record transactions. It could transform current systems, directly affecting professional accountants in accounting, auditing, tax, and consultancy services. It is not surprising that this system has caught the attention of the world's four largest accounting firms, Deloitte, EY, KPMG and PwC. Deloitte, for example, has set up a blockchain team of 800 professionals in 20 countries to develop

30 http://blokzincir.tubitak.gov.tr

applications in banking, cross-border payments, trade, and finance.[31]

The value of blockchain to accounting can be illustrated by the following example. In traditional accounting programs, a transfer amount sent to a customer can be recorded, changed, and deleted afterwards. In blockchain technology, the recording occurs at the time the transaction is made (by the real-time recording system), and it cannot be deleted or changed. The transaction is not recorded separately in the accounting system of either company; instead, it is recorded on a real-time encrypted shared system.

Blockchain can therefore improve the accuracy and efficiency of the invoicing and payment process, minimizing conflicts resulting from errors or missing invoices. With this technology, productivity will increase significantly, and the real-time recording system will enable records to be kept in a more transparent, secure, and cost-effective manner compared with conventional accounting technologies.

With a real-time recording system, there is also no need to wait for the end of the period or year for financial statements and reports. Currently, companies can announce their financial statements for the previous year in February at the earliest, but with this technology, they would be on our desks on the morning of January 1/New Year's Day.

With blockchain technology come **smart contracts**. Smart contracts are blocks of code written to automate certain processes that ensure contractual promises are fulfilled, monitored, and executed without the involvement of humans. For example, an employee's vacation earnings can be automatically paid off on a client's payroll following the dismissal of that person. When a smart loan agreement is made, the borrower's loan can be automatically deposited into the customer's bank account. Smart contracts automatically execute a wide variety of tasks when certain conditions are met.

Blockchain technology also allows financial statement users to

31 https://www2.deloitte.com/us/en/pages/financial-services/articles/blockchain-series-deloitte-center-for-financial-services.html/

access information faster, more efficiently and at an appropriate level. While corporate management and auditors may need full access to data in the distributed ledger system, for example, investors may only need access to high-level financial summary information and key financial metrics such as revenue growth, profitability, and earnings per share.

We can list the advantages of blockchain technology to the accounting profession as follows:

- Blockchain systems offer fast and powerful databases. Logging in and out of the system can be done faster and more efficiently compared with previous accounting software applications.
- It automates many accounting processes and reduces errors in data entries.
- Reconciliation processes become easier and automatic with smart contracts.
- Increases in the efficiency of blockchain accounting operations and decreases in errors will mean improved accounting processes at a reduced cost.
- The immutability of blockchain blocks makes it difficult for fraud and forgery; to change a record, one must simultaneously make changes on all copies of the distributed ledger, which is not possible. Blockchain also accelerates and shortens inspection processes. Many audit functions will be automated with smart contracts and auditors will spend less time checking records.
- It will be possible to instantly monitor assets such as stocks, cash values, funds, title deeds, and even inventory belonging to businesses.
- It will be possible to switch to a time-stamped and encrypted real-time recording system instead of retrospective recording in accounting applications.
- Confirmation and verification methods will disappear in audit practices, and absolute assurance will be given instead of reasonable assurance for financial statements.
- Conventional audits will be replaced by digital audits.

Finance executives on Wall Street believe that blockchain will become widespread across the entire financial sector. There is no doubt that this will be one of the biggest revolutions in the field of accounting after personal computers.

Radio Frequency Identification Technology (RFID)

Radio Frequency Identification is the general name given to technologies that are used to identify living things or objects with radio waves. In other words, it is the transformation of data carried by radio waves into information in a controlled working environment, and it can be used to track any object. RFID technology consists of four components: computer, RFID reader, RFID antenna and RFID tag.

RFID is one of the most important technologies of the twenty-first century because it enables real-time tracking of products in the supply chain. It is an automatic identification system consisting of a reader and a tag. Inside the tag, there is a microchip and an antenna that surrounds the microchip. Communication is established between the reader and the tag via electromagnetic waves. The electromagnetic waves emitted by the reader hit the chip as energy and activate it, and data is transferred from the tag to the reader. All this happens remotely and wirelessly. The reader converts the received data train into digital waveform and transfers it to the computer. Contactless credit cards, cards used to open doors and airline companies' luggage card applications are the best-known examples of this technology.

RFID offers an improved alternative to scanning barcodes which is a costly labor. Since collecting information through barcodes is expensive, retail companies only take inventory once or twice a year but can still get inaccurate data despite their costly efforts. Clothing stores' inventory accuracy is only around 65 percent, for example, and retailers are missing out on meaningful and high-volume data on re-stocking.[32]

However, these problems are easily overcome with RFID technology. Unlike barcodes, RFID is not restricted by field-of-view reading, and more than one RFID tag can be read at the same time. RFID tags can store critical information about a single item, they can be read in disorganized environments, and they can be reused as they have the potential to be overwritten multiple times. RFID allows automatic and instantaneous analysis to be implemented and automation of data collection for goods and services. This organizational and process-oriented efficiency provides guidance for decision-making on capacity aimed at increasing efficiency. Textile retailers, for example, could increase their annual revenues by at least 3% by using RFID.

Predominantly used in the consumer goods industry, RFID technology continues to evolve. RFID data is used for many different applications, including airline baggage tracking, electronic security, asset tracking and supply chain management. It is also used in the tracking of goods out of stock, product distribution, documentation, proof of delivery, asset management, product lifecycle tracking, recall management, product rotation, inventory and shipping accuracy, stock management, military applications, and the service industry. Meta (formerly Facebook) is developing RFID chips embedded in wristbands or badges to help its users perform various social networking tasks without the need for a computer or smartphone.

Walmart, one of the largest supermarket chains in the world, already uses RFID instead of barcodes in stock management, and does not have to use warehouses for its markets as a result. After products are read at the cash register and sold, they are automatically deducted from stock. The system automatically places orders with suppliers when product numbers decrease, and Walmart avoids a serious storage cost.

---

32 KARAER, O. MANAGING A RETAIL FASHION PRODUCT WITH RFID-ENABLED INVENTORY VISIBILITY. *Nigde Omer Halisdemir Universitesi Muhendislik Bilimleri Dergisi*, *8*(2), 796-809.

In terms of accounting, as companies adopt RFID over the next decade, computer systems will store cost data associated with each individual item of inventory and will be able to calculate finished inventory levels or cost of goods sold more accurately. Accountants will also be able to see changes in company procedures related to inventory management, and especially physical inventory, instantly and in real time. RFID technology has the potential to reduce costs and increase inventory management and accounting efficiency.

Big Data

"Big data" first appeared in the fields of astronomy and genetics but is now a general term used to refer to the collection, understanding, and processing of large amounts of data in digital environments. With the combination of machine learning and artificial intelligence technology, a large amount of information is arguably now produced autonomously by instruments. Big data organizes this collected data and helps businesses to understand and predict human behavior accordingly. This means the data owned by businesses can offer smarter management opportunities.

According to 2021 data, more than 500 hours of video is uploaded to YouTube every minute, an average of 682 million tweets are posted every day on Twitter, 2.9 million emails are sent per second, Instagram users upload more than 100 million photos and videos every day, and about 300 million people join social media every year. Facebook has an average of 1.58 billion active users, and more than 100 million messages are sent every minute worldwide via SMS and in-app messages. Today, more than 98 percent of stored information is electronic, and 90 percent of this data has been produced only in the last two years. These facts show what a huge amount of data we are dealing with. Big data is revolutionizing many fields, including business, politics, medicine, almost all-natural sciences, and social sciences.

The combination of big data and artificial intelligence will radically change the way we work. Human attributes such as experience and judgment will be replaced by predictions that can be derived from data. As businesses transform with the impact of big data and data analysis, the role of accounting and finance professionals is also changing. The accounting industry has already begun to take advantage of the opportunity provided by big data to improve efficiency and productivity in accounting practices.

Big data makes contributions to accounting applications through video, sound recordings and software. For example, the use of data obtained from RFID systems, which is a common source of big data, allows real-time stock costs to be seen. In fact, big data offers professional accountants the opportunity to take a leading role in problem-focused analysis.

Big data also enables companies to see challenges and disruptions in new ways, based on the analysis of all the data presented. This allows them to make a better evaluation of performance in management accounting and facilitates the budgeting process. It also helps detect deviations and irregularities in internal-external audits more efficiently. Finally, it allows a better assessment of items to be presented in financial reports and statements. Big data is a good and efficient tool that professional accountants can use to improve their accounting practices.

While conventional accounting data is mostly quantitative and structured, big data contains unstructured or semi-structured data that provides more supporting evidence and detail. Hence, big data needs to play an important role in the development of new accounting education programs; future accountants need to gain competence in using these new tools and processes to extract information from large volumes of data. With the right training, they will become successful at inferring correlations and conclusions for data that was previously incomprehensible with traditional tools such as spreadsheets. Big data will provide significant opportunities for accounting professionals in terms of data science, strategic planning, and implementation.

Three-dimensional Printing Technology (3D Printers)

Three-dimensional printers are devices that produce models designed and scanned in three dimensions, using many different materials, and without the need for extra molds or fixtures. Hospitals are already using 3D printers to create skeleton parts to use in the repair of human skulls, jaws, and limbs, etc, and 3D printing technology will play a key part in the future of manufacturing and distribution. It will be effective in every process of production, from design to storage, installation, and recycling, and it is expected to completely disrupt traditional factory production methods.

While conventional manufacturing tools are specifically designed to work with certain types of materials (e.g., plastic, aluminum, food materials, etc.), 3D printing technology offers a wider range of materials. These materials can be substituted for each other when the requirements for the product or available materials change. Preparation phases and production time in 3D printing technology can be much reduced compared with its factory counterparts, meaning products can be manufactured more quickly.

While the production industry will find cheaper manufacturing opportunities, and become more dynamic and flexible, 3D printing also offers individuals the ability to create cheap products at home. Instead of ordering the spare part needed to repair your suitcase or your car, for example, you will be able to easily print that part yourself. In the future, 3D printers could become just as common in people's homes as microwave ovens.

New accounting practices and fields of expertise will emerge in the future to meet the unique needs of this digital manufacturing industry. When the supply chain, production, marketing, and distribution models adapt to the new economy, the areas of auditing will expand. 3D printing technology will impact classical cost accounting methods at every level.

But this technology also raises important questions. 3D printing brings with it particularly complex global tax challenges: as it paves the way for international cooperation between individuals and companies, how and where will goods be taxed? And where will the intellectual property be stored? On the system on which it was designed, or where its components have been installed, or where the product has been printed?

This digital revolution has a high potential to reshape both manufacturing and accounting needs.[33]

- **Impact on cost accounting:** There is no doubt that 3D printing will significantly change the cost of production. Cost accounting will need to take into account the new efficiency of the digital manufacturing process for future operations.

- **3D printing may change the geography of supply chains:** 3D printers will eliminate the need to import a material you cannot obtain locally.

- **Customization:** 3D printing will allow the production of customized shapes and products. This flexibility will affect supply chains as well as manufacturers' stock procurements and cost-per-unit calculations.

- **Small-scale production:** 3D printing techniques allow the creation of an infinite number of small objects and parts. This may lead to unprecedented demand in the world of manufacturing and to new demand for complex parts.

- **Materials are changing:** Conventional production relies on machines designed to use specific materials on the production line. 3D printing offers a wider range of materials, which can be substituted if the cost or availability of the material, or the wishes of the manufacturer, change.

- **Waste effect:** 3D printing will minimize waste. Instead of cutting from a material with waste left over, we will be able to use only what is needed.

- **Changing the modern production line:** 3D printing technology will not require labor-intensive work on production lines; it will require a different skill set and often special training.

- **Change in labor costs:** In the last decade, cheap labor in Asia has seriously impacted global industry. Technologies like 3D printing can change this trend.

3D printers will certainly affect the accounting profession.

---

33 https://sldcpa.com/knowledge-insights/3d-printing-will-shape-future-manufacturing-accounting

Accountants need to be aware of how 3D printing technologies are changing cost models and making them increasingly dynamic and flexible, with an almost unimaginable variety of cheap production options becoming available. As key advisors to businesses, accountants must be equipped to inform their clients of the full benefits of 3D printing – not only in terms of lowering production costs, but also in terms of developing innovative new products and reducing negative impacts on the environment.[34]

Internet of Things (IoT)

The internet was, beyond argument, the most important technological development of the last century. So far, most of the information on the internet has been created by people to share with other people. Now, however, there are systems and devices that can communicate with each other through communication protocols and create smart networks by connecting to each other and sharing information.

The term "internet of things" was first coined in 1999 by Kevin Ashton during his employment at Procter & Gamble.[35] It was defined as "the worldwide network that uniquely addressable objects created among themselves and [the] communicating of these objects in this network with each other through a specific protocol". With this technology, any electronic device you can think of can access the internet and communicate with other devices.

Previously in production, a lot of people would spend a lot of time organizing and maintaining machinery and making sure everything was all right. Thanks to the internet of things, factories can respond to machine breakdowns much faster, automatically order parts when

34 Khazzam, R., E., (2015). 3D Printing Technology Shifts the Cost Modeling Game—What You and Your Clients Need to Know. IFAC URL: https://www.ifac.org/knowledge-gateway/preparing-future-ready-professionals/discussion/3d-printing-technology-shifts-cost-modeling-game-what-you-and-your-clients-need-know

35 Lueth, K. L. (2015). IoT basics: Getting started with the Internet of Things. *White paper*, 1-9.

needed, eliminate downtime, and save money and time overall. Without human intervention or interaction, this process can take place through systems involving interconnected devices, machines, and tools, etc. that exchange data over the internet.

How will IoT technology affect the accounting profession?

In the relatively near future, all devices and sensors will be equipped to connect to the internet, and businesses can take advantage of IoT to better understand and improve their products. How businesses collect this data, and the real-time information available through IoT, will transform many aspects of accounting and auditing, allowing better business planning and resource allocation.

The real-time data provided by IoT can help improve the accuracy of cost planning, forecasting, and budgeting. As the systems gain the ability to communicate, revenue and risk management also become easier. Losses from misconduct are minimized. Potential problems are identified earlier, and more appropriate responses to them can be found. We can expect many changes, particularly in auditing. IoT technology helps auditors and accountants to provide important information with meaningful, structured data collection and analysis.

Virtual Reality (VR) and Augmented Reality (AR)

Augmented reality is the enrichment of the physical environment in the real world with computer-generated sound, images, graphics, and GPS data, which we can feel and experience in real time.

One popular example is the Pokemon Go game application which became a phenomenon when it was released in 2016. In this app, players can see and collect virtual animated characters on their smartphones that appear to be integrated with the real world (as captured in real time by the smartphone's camera).

Virtual reality is the general term for content that can be played through devices such as head-mounted displays or smartphones. VR allows you to do many things in virtual worlds created by 3D computers. Walking on Mars, fighting on the front line in the Second

World War, flying a warplane, living the story of Batman through his eyes, or virtually painting with three-dimensional brushstrokes are just some of the things you can do with it.

The virtual and augmented reality market is expected to be worth $571.42 billion by 2025.[36]

How will virtual and augmented reality affect accountants?

A new generation of accounting software with augmented reality technology is coming into play to help accountants streamline and automate many of their tasks, such as updating data, preparing manual reconciliations, and generating reports. Augmented reality accounting can increase efficiency and organize processes safely. To facilitate accounting, it can be used to embed access to digital data in our view of the real world.

Accountants can use AR and VR technologies in areas such as education, meetings, and customer services. With augmented reality, an accountant can walk through the financial statements, move the figures with a finger or a nod, visualize graphs, and present different graphs in three dimensions showing how different situations might affect financial results. More realistic presentations can be made by combining digital and physical information in the accounting field with augmented reality. AR and VR technologies also provide significant cost savings in accounting applications.

Society 5.0

After Germany created Industry 4.0, Japan took digitalization one step further and introduced the concept of Society 5.0 – that is, technology for society. This is the fifth stage of human progression, after the hunter-gatherer, agriculture, industry, and information stages. Society 5.0 can be described as "the philosophy of creating a smart society that will properly manage technological power". Like

---

36 https://www.alliedmarketresearch.com/augmented-and-virtual-reality-market

Germany, Japan aims to transform its existing information society into a new super smart society.

Figure 5. Development and transformation of humanity

Japan's Society 5.0 program not only supports the economy, but also focuses on the opportunities that digitalization can create for society and individuals. As such, it has not limited digitalization to industry and management but is encompassing a strategy, policy and even a philosophy of national digital transformation. It encourages technology to be perceived not as a threat, but as an instrument that facilitates human life. The country aims to integrate Society 5.0 with all sectors and social activities with a view to providing economic development *and* solutions to big societal problems such as the aging world population, environmental pollution, and natural disasters. The essence of Society 5.0 is to find the most appropriate technological solution – such as artificial intelligence, robotics, and big data – to meet the needs of society and individuals.

Goals that the Society 5.0 philosophy aims to achieve:

- To develop solutions for the aging world population;
- To make the virtual world work together with the real world;
- To benefit from the internet of things by considering the interests of society;
- To create solutions for environmental pollution, climate crisis

and natural disasters.

Society 5.0 aims to eliminate regional, age, gender, and language differences, and to meet individual needs with fine-tuned products and services. Japan wants to cultivate new values through innovation and become a people-centered society where everyone can enjoy a high standard of life.

Digital transformation involves significant changes, both technologically and socially. Smart cities, smart homes, and smart factories will offer enormous opportunities to communities and individuals. Security, legal, privacy, and ethical issues need to be addressed to take full advantage of these opportunities. Society 5.0 could be the key to achieving a happier, more productive, inclusive, respectful, and environmentally friendly society in the future.

In 2019, IFAC (International Federation of Accountants) invited the G20 countries to pursue smart regulation, increased transparency, and inclusive growth. In its invitation, IFAC emphasized that these policies were actionable steps towards realizing the United Nations' Sustainable Development Goals (SDGs) as well as Japan's global vision for Society 5.0.[37] Certainly, Society 5.0's efforts to create a digital society will create further need for digital accountants.

Cyber Security

Cybercrime has emerged with the development of digital technology. It comprises activities that endanger the security of any information system, as well as crimes that are committed against the rights of individuals using information systems. Cyber security covers technologies, processes and controls designed to protect information systems, networks, and data from cyber-attacks.

Cybercrime and threats to information systems are a major concern globally. According to Cybersecurity Ventures, by 2025 the global

37 https://www.ifac.org/news-events/2019-06/tax-trade-and-transparency-dominate-g20-agenda-ifac-issues-call-action

cost of cybercrimes will reach $10.50 trillion.[38] American business magnate Warren Buffet considers cyber-attacks to be “a greater threat to humanity than nuclear weapons” and IBM president and CEO Ginni Rometty calls cybercrime the “greatest danger”. A single data breach resulting from cyber-attacks reportedly costs US companies more than $500,000 dollars on average.[39] Because of this, Big Four accounting firm PwC advises companies to implement best practice in cyber threat prevention even if not legally required to do so.

Undoubtedly, one of the accounting profession’s most important responsibilities is the protection and confidentiality of client data. As accountants collect and use increasing amounts of data, including customer information, they also meet new security risks. Accountants and financial institutions are very attractive to cyber criminals, and their intensive use of technology makes them a particular target. Email piracy is the most common type of cyber-attack, since many accounting offices use email to send tax documents and personal data to their clients. The server computers of accounting offices are also frequently hacked and held for ransom.

It is crucial to be aware of such cyber security risks and to learn how to take action against them. Everyone who works with accounting information systems needs training on cyber threats and the available security technology (virus detection, firewalls, etc.). As concerns about personal data ownership increase, it also becomes more and more important for professional accountants to establish a transparent exchange of value with clients for all kinds of data operations.

38 https://cybersecurityventures.com/cybercrime-damage-costs-10-trillion-by-2025/

39 https://www.varonis.com/blog/cybersecurity-statistics/

II.5-ACCOUNTANTS AND SKILLS IN THE DIGITAL AGE

Members of the accounting profession need to have certain qualifications to do their jobs in the best possible way. However, digitalization – brought about by the technologies and developments discussed in this chapter – is changing the qualifications generally expected of accounting professionals. A decade ago, a good professional accountant was expected to have tax knowledge, good writing technique, and a good memory – but today, with digital systems now automating accounting records and sending hand-filled statements straight to the relevant government department over the internet, these competencies are no longer particularly valued. Nowadays, the most sought-after competencies are the ability to actively use technology, the ability to master new systems of information and communication technologies, communication skills, and critical thinking. The lines between accounting and technology are getting fuzzier every day. It is therefore not surprising that organizations are looking for accountants who not only have accounting skills but also the technical skills needed in digital systems.

Accounting work is becoming automatic. Ready-made virtual accountants are available to small to medium-sized businesses via Intuit's Quickbooks, for example. These types of tools empower organizations and enable them to have more control over their accounting work – but they leave accountants needing to redefine their roles.

The Institute of Chartered Accountants in England and Wales recently listed the qualifications of the future professional accountant as follows:[40]

1. They are interested in new technologies. As innovations continue to advance complexity, accountants must stay up to date with the latest developments. They need to advise

40 https://www.icaew.com/learning-and-development/aca/aca-employers/the-future-professional

customers and businesses on how to get the most out of the latest technological advances from automation to blockchain, from big data to the cloud, and know how systems will work in the future.

2. They are powerful communicators. The ability to explain complex issues is something that successful accountants always need. A more complex world makes this talent more valuable.

3. They think flexibly. Although adaptability is among the characteristics of good accountants, it will be tested more than ever at this time of increasing change.

4. They think strategically. When routine and manual accounting practices become automated, they will need to be more practical. They will be asked to provide more value to the management board and senior staff through strategic advice and support.

5. They have global business connections. Accountants will remain at the heart of the global business community and will be central to building strong local economies around the world. To do this, they must continue to build and develop strong personal and business networks.

Accountants need to understand technological trends and take appropriate steps to adapt to them. The business world needs accountants who can go beyond traditional business processes to make use of digital technologies and adapt to developing methods. Accountants need to consider their role in this digital transformation and take action to prepare themselves for the digital future. Technology will continue to change at lightning speed, and basic IT skills are not enough. Accountants must be ready to integrate new and more efficient tools into existing processes. In particular, it is vital that professional organizations and universities create a competency map for future accountants and auditors. We must redesign the skills and equipment of professional accountants in order for them to be successful in the twenty-first century. We can list the basic skills that may be needed in this process as follows:

- **Analytical skills** Forward-looking accountants must have both a theoretical and practical understanding of data analytics. They must have the necessary knowledge to compile and analyze historical or current data, and knowledge of both predictive analysis and determinations of future financial returns.

- **Business intelligence** In the future, accountants will need to use their business acumen to develop financial solutions and to make contributions to their business at a strategic level. To adapt to the future, they will be required to have competency in data analysis, technology, and process design, as well as in data, project, and risk management.

- **Digital intelligence** Digital intelligence includes awareness and application of existing and emerging digital technologies, capabilities, practices, strategies, and culture. We cannot expect accountants to use the same software for the next 10 years; we must be ready to understand and use new developments.

- **Creativity** Creative thinking ensures that we will not be left behind in this exciting new era of digital discovery. Creativity in the accounting industry involves exploring potential results, establishing new connections, and generating new ideas. Technology opens many doors for new and improved processes.

- **Effective communication** Information is useless if it is not shared effectively. Analytical skills become dysfunctional if you cannot skillfully convey the information provided. Therefore, accountants should develop strong written communication skills to present their analysis in easy-to-understand documentation. Technology can do many things, but it cannot replace human interaction in business transactions.

- **Strategic decision-making** As many accounting operations will be handled by digital systems, accountants will have more time to make strategic decisions. Their participation in strategic decision-making processes in organizations is already increasing day by day. It will become more and more important to predict the future, guide the strategic planning process, guide decisions, manage risk and monitor performance.

CHAPTER III
DIGITAL TRANSFORMATION OF ACCOUNTING AND DIGITALIZATION

The twenty-first century has started a new technology age that reshapes daily life, facilitates conventional processes, and even provides opportunities for new business models. It is called “the age of digitalization”. Digitalization can be defined as the transfer of manually created data to a computer or digital environment. In other words, digitalization is the presentation of real information in a way that is not tied to a physical location. With the introduction of this concept in terms of the world of technology, the way has been paved for objects to access each other with the support of the internet, and without human intervention.

The mobile phone is the most symbolic invention of the digital age: not only it represents a revolution in itself, but also it is the intersection point of many other revolutions! Internet and ubiquitous networks; GPS and sensors; powerful cloud services that can transfer private information in real time and deliver customized content instantly; mass observation and the interconnection of billions of people and trillions of data points…

Digitalization is not just the fields where information can be stored and used; it is a technology that radically changes society and the world. The digitalization adventure that continues from the micro to macro level has spread over a wide area from individual to society, from end user to companies. It is possible to see its footprints in every conceivable field from education to health, from transportation to industry, from agriculture to mining.

With digitalization, some sectors have almost entirely abandoned their old business models. The music and broadcasting industry is moving to digital platforms. Radical changes have taken place especially in the field of industry. Again, the positive effects of digitalization can be seen more closely in service sectors such as health, banking, and education. As business and management models become more digital, business volumes are growing, employment areas are being created, and productivity and competitiveness are increasing. As technology develops, every object in direct contact with life is becoming digital.

Table 4. Role changes in professions with digitalization[41]

STABLE ROLES	NEW ROLES	UNNECESSARY ROLES
General Manager, CEO	Data analysts and scientists	Data entry personnel
Software and application development analysts	AI and machine learning experts	Executive secretaries
Data analysts and scientists	General manager, operations managers	Factory and assembly workers
Sales and marketing professionals	Big data analysts	Customer information and consumer services
Sales representatives	Digital transformation experts	Accountants and auditors
Human resources professionals	Sales and marketing professionals	Material registration and stock tracking officers
Finance and investment consultants	IT services	Financial analysts
Database and network professionals	Information security experts	Cashiers and ticket attendants
Risk management experts	Process automation specialists	Bank attendants
University and higher education teachers	Innovation professionals	Drivers
Energy and petroleum engineers	Robotics expertise and engineering	Door-to-door sales employees
Oil, natural gas operators	Community and cultural professionals	Statistics, finance, and insurance attendants
	Service and solution designers	Lawyers
	Digital marketing and strategists	

41 Turmob XX: Accounting Congress Presentation by Prof. Dr. Melih Erdogan 2018.

Digital transformation is not just about implementing a few random projects like updating a website or launching a mobile app. While analyzing the digital world, Tom Goodwin, Havas Media Strategist and Vice President of Innovation, says, "The world's largest taxi company Uber does not own a single vehicle. Facebook, the world's most popular media company, does not produce a single piece of content. AliBaba, the most valuable retailer, does not hold any stock. Airbnb, the world's largest accommodation provider, does not own any real estate. Something interesting is happening here."[42]

For this reason, adapting to digitalization and allowing change in our cultural structure will empower both societies and individuals.

Digital Transformation Philosophy

What are the prerequisites for digital transformation? People have always had to work in the face of an unpredictable future, but it is obvious that technology is evolving even faster than humanity's capability for easy adaptation. We are not just trying to adopt technology; we are also trying to understand the nature of change. Digital transformation is caused by the changing needs and expectations of consumers. Digital transformation is, therefore, a journey, not a destination. We need instruments to accompany us on this journey.

For instance, we need philosophy in the digital age more than ever. Philosophy is the compass of human civilization. It is the knowledge and understanding of the mind. Philosophy can help us face the most critical challenges of digital transformation.

Agility is important because it requires both structural and psychological change. It means taking risks, changing, and investing in it. Businesses and people who embrace change and adapt to a more agile model have the potential to be more successful than ever. An agile business means a business that understands social, environmental, technological, and procedural issues.

42 Goodwin, T. (2017). The battle is for the customer interface (2015).

Digital transformation is a revolution for business models and offers two options for businesses: adapt or stay behind. It invites us to look beyond our comfort zone, and it is worrisome for some, while exciting for others. Digital transformation offers opportunities, but it, by any account, cannot be stopped.

Digital transformation cuts us off from the past, but we allow it within the strategy we determine. It is, essentially, about creating an integrated technology platform that reinvents all organizational processes. It is the step that lets you aim for a bigger goal for digitally transforming the product, changing your mode of operation, and connecting with your customers in a different way. You can think of this as a change in business philosophy.

Regardless of department or process, all data and analytics focus on one thing: business development. A successful digital transformation lies not in the application of new technologies; but instead in enabling businesses to take advantage of the new possibilities offered by technology.

As conventional business models change, design is emerging as one of the important components. Engineers are motivated by working on problems, challenging them: "How can I make this machine run?", "How can I generate energy at the most affordable cost?" The method engineers need to invent, design, and test these processes is the design thinking.

Digital transformation presents us with complex and undefined problems. The "Design- Thinking" methodology is an effective way to tackle the problems posed by this transition. It provides in-depth information on digital transformation needs and requirements. It is a practical and creative method to solve developing problems, especially in areas such as engineering and architecture. Design Thinking is useful for rebuilding business models that require innovative solutions, as it is a powerful tool for handling unknown works or tasks that have never been done before.

As we have seen in the efforts for conventional change, communication also plays a crucial role in digital transformation. Digital transformation is the transition of a business from conventional processes to digital functions, which are more based on technology. Digital transformation represents the departure of conventional businesses from the way they usually operate. As a result of research by the international management consultants McKinsey & Company, the requirements for successful digital transformation are listed as follows: [43]

- Preparing plans and roadmap for the long-term sustainability of change,
- Determining change priorities,
- Being open to change,
- Being transparent and accountable,
- Continuous improvement and development of the transformation process,
- Effective management of the digital transformation program,
- Providing adequate resources to implement transformation and change.

As digital technologies are reshaping the industry, many companies are trying to sustain a large-scale change to capture the benefits of these trends or simply keep up with their competitors. In 2020 alone, a sum of over 1.3 trillion dollars was spent on digital transformation projects around the world, and this figure is expected to double to nearly $2.3 trillion by 2023.[44] Research on digital transformation shows that the global success rate of transformation efforts is low. Only 16 percent of survey respondents say their organizations have successfully improved digital transformation performance and equipped them to sustain changes over the long term. 88 percent of the companies believe they do not have the right technology to

---

43 https://www.mckinsey.com/business-functions/mckinsey-implementation/our-insights/how-the-implementation-of-organizational-change-is-evolving#

44 Dibbern, J., & Hirschheim, R. (2020). Introduction: Riding the waves of outsourcing change in the era of digital transformation. In Information Systems Outsourcing (pp. 1-20). Springer, Cham.

implement a digital strategy at the moment. 59 percent of companies say they worry that they may be too late to start digital transformation efforts and that they may fall behind their competitors[45]. For example, Ford has a long and successful track record of selling vehicles around the world, but we can say that is what makes it difficult to bring about a digital transformation that could fundamentally change company operations that have developed over 115 years.[46]. On the other hand, a significant part of Tesla's success can be attributed to the highly effective implementation of digital transformation along the entire value chain. Using technology, they developed a complete digital ecosystem of integrated products, services, and operational capabilities to lead a customer-centric strategy.[47]

Even high-tech media and telecom industries are struggling for digitalization. The success rate of these industries does not exceed 26 percent. In more conventional industries such as oil and gas, automotive, infrastructure and pharmaceuticals, the digital transformation is even more challenging. Success rates in these industries range from 4 to 11 percent. Success rates also vary according to company size. Organizations with less than 100 employees are 2.7 times more likely to achieve a successful digital transformation than organizations with more than 50,000 employees.[48] In conclusion, the organizational transformation required to invest in digital technologies and realize the promises is critical not only for the success of businesses and professions but also for their individual professional lives.

Smart Factories

Since the first industrial revolution, efforts have been made to remove human labor from production and to replace human labor with smart systems. In the twentieth century, machines and robots

45 Morgan, B. (2019). 100 Stats on Digital Transformation and Customer Experience. Forbes.

46 https://www.raconteur.net/digital/digital-transformation-failure/

47 https://www.thefuturefactory.com/blog/tesla

48 https://www.technologymagazine.com/data-and-data-analytics/mckinsey-unlocking-success-digital-transformations

began to lift weights that people could not handle and make assembly work on the production line that could not be done by workers. With the added processing and control of digitized data in the twenty-first century, they are being used in many areas. Even though robots do not have the ability to think, they have begun to learn. We can trace the dream of building a machine that can genuinely think back to 1950. The article on the artificial intelligence discipline published by Alan Turing that year was a milestone in artificial intelligence.

Smart factories are the name of a flexible system that can self-optimize its performance over a wider network, adapt to new conditions, learn, and carry out production processes autonomously. Data collected in the smart factory is transparent. Real-time data visualizations can be used in decision-making autonomy for managers by transforming data obtained from spatial or production products. A transparent network can provide greater visibility throughout the facility. They provide businesses with tools such as role-based views, real-time alerts, notifications, and real-time monitoring to enable them to make more accurate decisions. This makes it predictable to keep necessary inventory in stock or replenish it and to identify quality issues. Thus, security and maintenance processes can be followed. Smart factories' predicting future results based on historical and real-time data can increase uptime, productivity, and quality, and prevent safety problems.

In the past thirty years, large parts of the British manufacturing industry have turned to China, India, and Eastern Europe. With automation, it will become financially feasible to bring them all back. Robots do not want money; they do not sleep, and they can work in the dark.

Digital transformation technologies have the potential to completely transform productive labor. Smart algorithms and big data may replace qualified knowledge workers. Robots are likely to be used in manufacturing environments – at least partially and inexpensively – that have resisted automation until now.

Digital transformation is critical for the success of professions and business models. Industry 4.0 is the only way to guarantee your future in the industry. The digital transformation trends driving Industry 4.0

are just the first steps taken towards the future. I am confident that the more the technology evolves, the further it will take us. But now is the time to take the necessary steps to make sure we are ready for digital transformation in our professions and business models.

III.1-FUTURE OF THE ACCOUNTING PROFESSION IN THE LIGHT OF DIGITALIZATION

The Economist magazine published a study on the professions that computerization will bring to an end in the next ten years, and accounting is among the top professions that will disappear.[49]

Oxford University lecturer and author Daniel Susskind's article titled "We All Know of the End of the Accounting Profession" draws attention to the change the profession will experience in the future. Muhammad Azizul Islam also states in his article "The Future of the Accounting Profession" that the accounting profession will face important changes in the coming years and that academics and members of professional organizations should respond to this change.

International accounting firms are spending money on developing high-tech auditing tools in areas such as cloud systems, digitalization, and technological change to evaluate the future opportunities and risks of the accounting profession. KPMG and IBM Watson's "Artificial Intelligence Unit" project can be cited as an example[50].

The Ministries of Finance state that due to the change and transformation to be experienced in the field of information technologies, that therefore a lot of information, and statements they will need in the future will be automatically and instantly recorded by digital systems. These digital systems will be as easy and simple as social media applications ordinary people use.

Some of the most important projects in the field of accounting still relate to the tax system (excluding basic tax statements and electronic government applications). If these projects continue to be implemented, members of the accounting profession will be

---

49 https://www.economist.com/business/2019/06/27/will-a-robot-really-take-your-job

50 Melendez, C. (2016). Artificial intelligence gets into auditing, what's next. *Infoworld.com*.

responsible for the accuracy of the information produced by the information and automation systems instead of making statements and notifications. The accountants of the future will be independent from their offices, keeping in constant contact with their customers and providing guidance for them for their futures.

Digitalization and the e-transformation process are the foundation of the transition from product-oriented concept to information-oriented concept. Easy access to information has also positively affected the accounting industry. Accounting has a decisive role in the equality, transparency, accountability, and responsibility of corporate governance. It must be able to use information in a timely and correct manner to determine local and global competition strategy. One of the most important contributions of digitalization to the accounting profession may be the prevention of accounting errors.

The effects of technological developments and digitalization on the accounting profession in the near future are expected to be as follows:

- The work done by accounting professionals will be performed by digital systems,
- The conventional accounting education, which includes financial accounting, auditing, and tax preparation, will be replaced by an education system based on accounting technologies within the framework of digitalization and e-transformation,
- Accountants will need new competencies and skills,
- Accountants will be required to have effective experience in information technologies rather than just knowledge of tax regulations and interpreting tax laws,
- Technological developments will offer new opportunities and new career fields for accountants,
- Consultancy and auditing functions will become prominent in the accounting profession,
- All accounting systems will be transformed into cloud systems, and it will be easier to access information whenever and wherever wanted,

• It will be possible to utilize savings from costs such as storage and record keeping, conventional methods will be eliminated, all operations will be performed over barcode systems and internet-based accounting (cloud and Blockchain systems),

• The importance of cyber-attack measures, information security and user privacy will increase in the accounting industry,

• Accountant's roles and job descriptions will change radically,

• Part-time virtual accountants will emerge, who will offer high-value services to businesses, rather than full-time accountants,

• More digital tools will be used, effectiveness and efficiency will increase, thanks to digitalization,

• With blockchain technology, the conventional ledgers in accounting will be replaced with digital ledgers,

• Real-time recording systems will come into use instead of a retrospective recording system in accounting applications. It will be possible to view financial statements and reports instantly.

The modern world we live in is full of new ideas and interesting technologies, and it is a constant journey to discover how we can turn these digital tools into advantage. Today, academics, professional organizations, and professional accountants say that a digital storm is approaching, but none of them offer sufficient recommendations or solutions on how to protect ourselves from this storm.

Today, the Covid-19 pandemic is forcing accountants to make radical changes and transform in many areas from business practices to working conditions, from skill sets to continuous professional development training and accounting practices. One of the topics that accountants around the world are most curious about is the issue of how the accounting profession will be shaped after Covid-19.

My recommendation is the redesign of the accounting profession in order to better cope with global crises such as Covid-19 as well as the technological changes it will experience. At this point, the "accounting engineering model" may be a solution proposal.

III.2-THE EFFECTS OF DIGITALIZATION ON ACCOUNTING EDUCATION

It can be misleading to define digital transformation by focusing on evolving technology. Digital transformation is a transition period in an historical process. This period presents changes and continuities between both old and new forms of accounting. As accounting practices become more digitally based, accounting education should turn from verbal culture to a digital and analytical culture.

Even though accounting has a great technological foundation, universities and educational institutions basically approach accounting education from a theoretical point of view, without including modern information systems and technologies. Therefore, they do not graduate students with the necessary technological skills demanded by the market, whereas in accounting education, new technology and social changes are required to support the student's learning development. For this reason, it is necessary to encourage new interdisciplinary tools that teachers and students receive in the field of accounting with the application of information and communication technology in the classroom and in accounting education processes.

The question that arises here is what are the informatics competencies that help professional accountants do their jobs better? A commission established under the leadership of the American Institute of Financial Advisors and composed of academics, conducted research on the follow-up of the accounting curriculum of the future. Table 5. gives the rankings of the best twenty-five technologies that were identified according to the results of this research, for the technology competence of future accounting professional candidates.

Table 5. 25 technologies for the technology competence of accounting professionals[51]

Ranking	Technology	Ranking	Technology
1	Electronic spreadsheets	14	Query languages
2	Business intelligence and analytics technologies	15	Big Data technologies
3	Database management software	16	Diagramming software
4	Enterprise resource planning (ERP) software	17	Internet research software
5	Accounting and tax research software	18	Network technologies
6	Security technologies	19	Reporting software
7	Communication software	20	Tax preparation software
8	General ledger software	21	XBRL (eXtensible Business Reporting Language)
9	Word processing software	22	Privacy technologies
10	Cloud computing	23	Application integration technologies
11	Generalized audit software	24	Programming languages
12	Governance, risk management and compliance (GRC) software	25	Mobile technologies
13	Presentation software		

51 The Pathways Commission, "In Pursuit of Accounting's Curricula of the Future", 2015, pp. 23-24

Digital transformation is inevitable in the future of accounting. This also applies to accounting education. It is very important for the future of accountants to include more technology and numerical courses in accounting education, as well as in professional competence courses.

Employment of professional accountants in the future will only be possible when they have the skills required by the digital world.

Innovative technology can provide a better policy formation, more sustainable business model, new jobs, and more revenue opportunities for accounting. So, how will professional accountants acquire the right skills they will need to advance their careers? In fact, the extent to which professional accounting institutions and accountants adopt technological innovation will play a critical role in determining the problem. As the role of the modern accountant evolves, those who find new ways of change in business life, those who have the motivation to move forward, and those with an open mind will be more advantageous. Those who analyze the results well, who can think critically, who have professional judgment and strategic decision-making skills, and those who learn coding languages and effective communication will come to the forefront.

The main principle for accountants is that they help businesses understand the future possibilities of accounting and how to move in new directions, rather than just reacting and fulfilling their clients' wishes.

While conventional accounting tends to view accountants' roles as only a theoretical role, accounting engineers may assume leadership roles more comfortably.

We should not forget that accounting, which is a profession full of tradition and surrounded by regulatory challenges and concerns, must work hard to embrace, and respond proactively to the opportunities and challenges of the digital revolution. In order to respond to barriers to innovation with agility, all parties to accounting must have a forward-looking mindset.

III.3-WHAT HAPPENS IF THE ACCOUNTING PROFESSION CANNOT MAKE THE DIGITAL TRANSFORMATION?

Consider how much the accounting profession has changed from the pen-bookkeeping days to the present. Accountants have constantly transformed themselves and kept up with the times since the birth of professional accounting in Venice in the fifteenth century. Technology is blurring the boundaries of the accounting profession, expanding the scope of work for accountants, and presenting them new threats and opportunities. In my opinion, the theory of the end of accounting means a less perceptible, constantly evolving, and digitized accounting profession that requires less energy compared to current accounting practices. So, what if the accounting profession fails to make this digital revolution?

Accounting candidates are still receiving extensive training in conventional accounting practices such as the uniform chart of accounts and journal entry; but they scarcely need them for accounting any longer. Members of the profession neither make an accounting record nor write a ledger. All of these are done automatically by accounting programs. Accounting technologies, especially those that have entered among accounting practices over the last ten years, are often not included in accounting education.

As digital systems take over the work of accountants, the need for accountants will decrease. Employers who will employ accountants in the future will especially prefer professional accountants who are able to make analysis, comments, and consultation, develop strategies, have knowledge of information and communication technology systems, have communication and critical thinking skills, and can use technology actively.

If transformation cannot be made in line with technological developments, we will face a serious army of unemployed accountants in the coming years. If we cannot meet the needs of the future business life, alternative professionals who can meet these requirements will be preferred instead of accounting professionals. They may be financiers, bankers, strategy experts, software engineers, statisticians, and data engineers.

The importance of transformation and change is obvious. In addition, there will be serious costs and consequences for not achieving this transformation. Ibn Rushd, one of the most intelligent and creative people in world history, said: "If the egg is broken from the outside, life ends; if it is broken from the inside, life begins; because important transformations always start from within." Based on this philosophy, if the accounting profession fails to transform, it may disappear.

What can be done for digital transformation?

• We must honestly and openly admit the background changes in our policies and professional discourse.

• Any discussion and potential for accounting must be open for redesigning.

• We must approach every aspect of the digital transformation challenge systematically. Because new and creative thinking can emerge from systematic approaches and from more stakeholders.

• Accounting institutions must make digital transformation a matter of vision. Necessary actions must be taken with the logic of "thinking ahead, thinking again".

• It is important how we engage in constructive discussions, how we proactively investigate diversity and how we avoid blind spots in the digital transformation process.

• Most importantly, we must be able to develop a digital transformation strategy that aims at taking advantage of the opportunities and effects of new technologies in a faster, better, and more innovative way.

Members of the accountant profession must be open to changes, avoid defending the status quo, and attach importance to lifelong learning. We must stay up-to-date and learn how to identify opportunities that can help improve the accounting practice process.

Digital Transformation Strategy

At the first glance, it may seem difficult to redesign a profession in the framework of digital transformation. It is imperative that digital transformation be carried out within the framework of a strategy. This strategy must be based on the vision of where the accounting profession should be in the future. Digital transformation strategy begins with answering basic questions, such as what, why, how, and who. It bridges the current situation with the desired long-term plan. The most important step of this strategy is to be open to change.

To implement the digital transformation strategy, professional accountancy organizations must steer the change correctly. Professional organizations must be at the forefront in embracing transformation and motivate professionals to be technology savvy.

Once the digital vision is determined, strategy must be implemented to achieve this vision, and for this, the parties of accounting must be on the same boat. Achieving the technology must not be the final goal, but instead, technology must be used as a tool to achieve the strategy. In general, the strength of a digital transformation strategy lies in its objectives and goals.

A creative approach in redefining business models is needed. Also needed is a digital transformation strategy for developing how processes, information structure, systems and how members of the professional community will interact and improving usability. You must see exactly what you want to achieve and the steps you plan to take to achieve it. Those who are successful in digital transformation have a clear and strategic vision on knowing how to transform technology and apply what is needed.

Digital transformation is difficult, because necessary changes must be made in almost every field of the professions to be successful. These changes will not happen overnight, so it is helpful to think of digital transformation as a journey rather than a destination.

Digital transformation enables an organization to compete better in an ever-changing economic environment as technology advances. For this purpose, transformation is necessary for any business or non-profit organization that wants to survive in the future.

III.4-ACCOUNTING INDUSTRY OF THE FUTURE

People will probably consume more resources and lead a more technologically advanced life in the future. It is certain that they will live longer and remain healthier compared to today. In the future, technology will make our life easier and save more of them, too… Smart cities, automated cars, robots, 3D printers in every home, space tourism, artificial intelligence systems in all areas of life, asteroid mining, synthetic biology, and virtual reality will be present in our lives. So, what awaits the accounting industry in the future?

The future of the accounting profession will be built on digitalization and applications. The emergence of virtual accountants, the replacement of public institutions such as physical tax offices or social security institutions with virtual public institutions, artificial intelligence accounting systems that can make their own decisions, hologram systems making it unnecessary for the taxpayers to go to tax offices to fulfill their tax duties, accounting programs communicating with people and machines, data analysis for members of the accounting profession, strategy and consultancy tasks coming to the forefront, digital audits, the use of blockchain and cloud system technologies, these are some of the changes that may be experienced in the accounting industry of the future…

In the future, it will be almost impossible to find accountants who perform accounting with conventional accounting methods. All of the conventional operational processes of accounting such as registration, declaration and cost calculation will be performed by artificial intelligence systems. These systems can be expected to make decisions on their own, control and work in integration with production lines.

All audit processes are expected to be digitized in the future. Digitalization in the audit process will help increase assurance by placing digital traces of when and by whom each file was accessed. The efficiency and accuracy of digital inspections will be increased. Audit procedures will be applied to 100 percent of the records instead of by sampling method and absolute assurance will be given for the authenticity of financial statements instead of reasonable assurance.

The way of doing business and job descriptions of members of the accounting profession will change with artificial intelligence, robotics and Blockchain technology. Since most of the work of accountants will be done by artificial intelligence systems in the future, accountants are expected to turn to more specific jobs such as consulting, top-level management developing strategy, and digital auditing. It is considered that the successful accountants of the future will be strong communicators and people with high technological skills and strategic visions.

In the future, there will be factories that will detect almost everything that occurs within it, consisting of a highly connected ecosystem that offers state-of-the-art solutions. In the smart factories of the future, there will be a digitally controlled and managed setting that will monitor all production information and receive data from robots and machine monitors in real time.

It will be possible to monitor assembly lines in real time by means of a cloud system in smart factories. Thus, it will be possible to change the plans of the lower functions of the value chain at any time. Factories will be remotely operated via mobile devices, including smartphones and tablets. Smart factories will make the work of accountants easier. As the smart factories will manage their own stocks, create new orders automatically, calculate costs instantly and in real time, accountants will be able to turn to more value-added jobs.

In the future, retrospective recording will be replaced by a real-time recording system. Tax will be calculated by artificial intelligence systems and reported to virtual tax offices instantly at the time of spending. Thus, companies will be able to see their profit, loss, and payable tax amount instantly. Many of today's statements and notifications will become useless and complex tax statement systems and applications will be replaced by simpler tax and accounting practices. It will be possible to make tax inspections and audits instantly.

It can be predicted that public institutions such as tax offices and social security institutions that exist physically today, will be replaced by virtual institutions and virtual civil servants. All physical transactions such as tax payment and petition will be done with the hologram system.

Digital systems will be able to check all records in a short time; thereby tax crimes such as tax evasion and money laundering will be reduced or will be detected in a truly short time. It is also possible that the unregistered economy will disappear completely, and tax injustice will be eliminated.

Accounting and tax calculations will be simplified. Tax inspections and audits will be done instantly, so there will be no need for complex tax laws and practices.

Hologram technology is expected to be used extensively in almost every field of accounting, from accounting education to application and tax collection. Accounting students will be able to listen to lessons from teachers with the hologram method. A taxpayer who wants to pay his tax will be able to handle all tax transactions with the hologram system without going to the tax office.

There are two ways to confront the future for the accounting profession: the future can be allowed to arrive passively, or studies that will benefit the future of the accounting profession can be shaped around opportunities. At this point, the future of the profession is in the hands of idealist members of the accounting profession, professional organizations, and academics under the guidance of the knowledge and technology that the twenty-first century will offer.

With digitalization, members of the accounting profession will be able to attract more customers and offer them more added value. I have some recommendations for them to embrace the future and technological changes:

- Professional organizations should encourage accountants to technological innovations and support these innovations,
- Cyber risks should be taken seriously, and they should be planned ahead,
- A new modeling should be studied for the digital revolution of accountancy,

- Digital systems should be used in all areas of the accounting industry,
- Accounting industry should have a more agile workforce with technological skills,
- The infrastructure of the accounting industry should be ready for the digital revolution,
- Accounting professionals should learn correct and effective communication,
- Accounting professionals should be allowed to make analysis and consult,
- Accountants should improve themselves in the areas of critical thinking, emotional intelligence, creativity, strong presentation, and communication skills, as well as engineering skills.

III.5-ARE YOU READY FOR THE DIGITAL ACCOUNTING OF THE FUTURE?

In their book "The Future of the Professions", Richard and Daniel Susskind explain how technology will transform the human workforce and professions, especially in sectors of health, clergy, law, journalism, management consulting, architecture, tax, and accounting. The book emphasizes the role of artificial intelligence and digital platforms on the change of professions. The authors are both optimistic and pessimistic about the future of professions. The book describes systems that are likely to replace old professions, providing a fascinating glimpse into the changes that have already happened or have not happened yet.

Interesting notes about the future of the professions in the book are as follows:

- Artificial intelligence machines, working independently or by non-expert users, will take over many of the routine tasks that do not require expertise. This will lead to the extinction of conventional professions.

- Machines can perform better than humans. For centuries, doctors, accountants, lawyers, teachers, and architects have solved problems that were too complex for most of us. Doctors, accountants, teachers, architects, consultants, and lawyers are at the top of the list of the professions that digital transformation will change the way of doing business in the 21st century.

- There are two possible future scenarios for professions: the first one being technology accelerating the conventional way of working and optimizing it (Like architects using computer aided software) and the second where it will be finding completely new ways of solving problems through technologies, for which our professions are the only solution. Rather than seeing the doctor on Skype, artificial intelligence systems looking at medical diagnoses could be a new way of delivering professional service. This is a method that threatens the professions.

- Technology is actively changing the work of conventional professions. Over time, most of the work done by accountants will be done by either different people, "self-learning systems" or both.

I certainly hope that the second scenario will create an environment where our professions exist traditionally and where we can access solutions to problems more easily and with less cost. As the famous economist John Maynard Keynes said, "The difficulty lies, not in the new ideas, but in escaping the old ones...."

All professions are working hard to implement digital transformation. Professions that have not started to build technical infrastructure and data analysis capabilities, which are the lifelines of digitalization, will not be able to achieve this. Adopting and integrating digital and physical technologies that exist today improves accountancy's productivity and also lays the foundation for future innovation and growth.

According to the findings I have obtained within the scope of my research, professional accountants are aware of digital change and support it and they say that they will strive to adapt. However, this process is not as easy as it seems.

In the digitalization journey, there is a need for a new model that will improve the accounting profession, transform it, and make it get results. This model needs to integrate the accounting profession with digitalization in all areas such as education, culture, and practice. The solution is recommended as the "accounting engineering model" in this book.

The accounting engineering model, which will make use of information and communication technologies as an effective tool, will transform the accounting profession from verbal culture to digital culture. Engineering skills will contribute to professional accountants in subjects such as reading, making analysis, interpreting digital data, problem recognizing and solving, and developing strategies. The accounting engineering model will take the accounting profession far beyond conventional methods such as recording, reporting, and making statements. Accounting professionals will be able to manage data easily by adapting to digital systems such as e-applications.

Accounting engineering will provide members of the accounting profession with the competence to read, understand, use, manage and critically evaluate digital systems. In this way, the digital revolution will bring benefits and opportunities to the accounting profession.

Engineering is the ability to think through mathematical logic and it is a process of systematic thought. Today, engineers address social issues such as inequality, poverty, and climate change – beyond building and designing. For example, it is now concerned with environmental engineering, social engineering, risk engineering and change engineering. Accounting engineering was born in the light of this vision. In the twenty-first century, professionals who are trained as accounting engineers or who improve themselves in technological fields and have engineering skills will be preferred and both the status and earnings of the members of the profession will be positively affected. Their competence in the execution of their professions will increase, and accounting will become more efficient.

Accounting engineers will be specialized in their fields and will combine their theoretical and practical knowledge with mathematics, philosophy, and science. Accounting engineering will provide professional career fields that are redesigned according to global developments. The positive aspect of accounting engineering is that it will enable the members of the accounting profession to assume a more central and strategic role in businesses. Accounting engineers will provide opportunities for professionals to do higher-level, value-added business in the financial practices of businesses. Thereby, accountants will gradually become strategic business advisors.

In conclusion, instead of being scared by technology, professional accountants should seize the opportunity that the new world offers. At this point, the cooperation of universities, public institutions, professional organizations, and accountants is important. In particular, reshaping the educational process is of critical importance.

Training needs to be made richer with digital systems. It must have a focus on skills that are presently acquired through experience.

CHAPTER IV
ACCOUNTING ENGINEERING

IV.1-CREATIVE THINKING METHODOLOGY AND INNOVATION

How do you think the people who changed the world, people like Steve Jobs, Jeff Bezos, and Elon Musk, became prominent figures among millions of people? Their innovative and creative thinking skills make them distinctive. Innovators change the status quo and are not afraid to take risks, to create change and to make an impression. Indeed, the greatest innovators emerge from those who learn from different fields and turn what they learn into extraordinary things.

Steve Jobs made a technological revolution with his unprecedented emphasis on aesthetics and user friendliness. Jeff Bezos said, "What's dangerous is not to evolve..." One of Elon Musk's best pieces of advice was to be "constantly think about how you could be doing things better and questioning yourself." Many studies put forward that the innovative mind is not innate and can be developed through observation and thinking techniques. The truth is that innovators are successful because they have an innovative mind.

Innovative people are good at problem solving and they also have a vision. The most innovative people in the world are the most curious ones; they ask a lot of questions and always seek ways to improve things. Steve Jobs was great at discovering innovations based on existing products such as laptops, mobile phones, and music players. He did not invent these products; he used innovation correctly to make them better and more useful.

A curious mind likes to get to know both familiar and unknown things. We can define curiosity as a hunger for exploration. Curiosity includes tendencies such as intellectual flexibility, openness, honesty, doing new things and being ready to try new alternatives. It encourages and develops critical and creative thinking.

For most people it is difficult to question the status quo. Innovators, on the other hand, do not settle for the status quo and like to challenge what is considered as norm or standard. For example, if Elon Musk had listened to the people around him, he would not have. He was not afraid to take risks and made many of his dreams, which were said to be impossible, come true. He sold his first video game at the age of 12. He co-founded and leads several technology companies such as Tesla Motors, PayPal, and SpaceX. He is an innovator and possesses the courage and creative abilities necessary to realize his dreams.

Creative persons have the ability to design new ways to accomplish tasks, solve problems, and deal with challenges. Creativity is being able to see connections that others cannot and to think of new things that they do not. You cannot create space for innovation in business models without finding a way to improve your innovation and creativity skills. Whether you invent a new product or find a solution to a problem, what you need is to acquire an innovative and creative thinking skillset. Before you can create something original and different you need to be able to seek a connection between the existing scenarios and abstract ideas and facts.

Innovation comes from creativity; creativity connects different ideas and facts together. According to Amazon's founder Jeff Bezos, trials are key to innovation, and innovators see the world as a laboratory. In 1994, before the internet became valuable, Bezos came across an article stating that the internet is growing 2300 percent a year. Instead of ignoring the statistics, he asked himself, "What kind of business opportunity does this new thing called the Internet offer?" Bezos then set up an innovative business process for delivering goods, and "the world's largest shopping site" was born.

It requires a different way of thinking to connect different fields, put big ideas into action, solve global problems and imagine one step ahead. One thing that sets innovators apart from the pack is that they are not afraid of making mistakes. All the barriers in front of you make it more important to maintain your faith and focus. Some people might call it pure optimism or unrealistic idealism, but productive innovators like Thomas Edison and others had to go through thousands of unsuccessful ways before they managed to invent the light bulb. Innovators like him see their mistakes as an opportunity to perfect their innovations.

Many products we see today are the result of putting two or more ideas or concepts together. The best example of such innovative inventions is the smartphone, which is basically integrated with advanced computing capabilities and internet connectivity.

It was quite difficult to imagine Google, which was built on the internet search algorithm, 30 years ago. Tomorrow's Google will be built on technology that looks like science fiction today. The ability to apply innovative thinking in the digital environment has become a characteristic of successful people. We need creative, innovative, and critical thinking to respond to the new business models of the twenty-first century. Tomorrow's successful professions will rely on new ideas and creative thinking rather than improving old processes.

Google asks its employees to devote at least 20 percent of their time to creative thinking and innovation work. For this reason, it improves the working space and conditions for its employees, organizes trips for its teams, offers financial incentives, provides its employees with the opportunity to attend conferences led by important CEOs, as well as providing gym classes, and even allows employees to bring their pets to the office. The only purpose for doing these is to enhance their employees' creative thinking and innovation skills.

Today's world uses the latest technology to design and analyze innovative and creative thinking solutions. With innovations such as the Internet of Things (IoT), robots, fast modeling, artificial intelligence and big data analysis, people create thousands of innovations by collaborating with smart machines. Not only do intelligent machines perform routine tasks of humans more efficiently, but they are also trained to work with human intelligence.

Some patterns and traditional thinking methods must be abolished for business models of the twenty-first century. Digital transformation is best expressed in the mind that appreciates criticism, that is ready for new solutions and ideas, and that is not afraid to evaluate ideas. In the digital transformation process, we can achieve great success by facing challenges and responding to them with our new thoughts and self-confidence. Creative and innovative thinking are essential requirements for the improvement of professions, especially in digital transformation.

Imagination is more important than information. Information is limited, whereas imagination embraces the whole world, encourages progress, and gives birth to evolution. Would you like to be someone who pioneers this change with new and effective ideas?

As it is often said, “The definition of insanity is doing the same thing over and over and expecting different results”. If we need to have different experiences and learn different things, then we must try different things. We need to unleash the potential of the innovative mind of man, too. Creativity is the key to success in these areas. We must direct ourselves to lifelong learning and developing a creative mind. Our life probably will not be enough to achieve this, so we must get started as early as possible. Yes, we can rebuild the accounting profession now.

IV.2-AN INTERDISCIPLINARY APPROACH IN ACCOUNTING, ENGINEERING, AND INFORMATION TECHNOLOGIES TO DEVELOP THE 21ST CENTURY SKILLS OF ACCOUNTANTS

Global crises such as Covid-19 encourage scientists, healthcare professionals, political analysts, economists, and business leaders to share their experiences and to collaborate. No discipline alone can address all the problems associated with the challenges of global crises and produce solutions for these problems.

This is also true for accounting science. We can say that accounting alone is not enough for the solution of multidimensional economic transactions and events of the twenty-first century.

The reason for this is that an interdisciplinary approach uses multiple ideas and research methods. It can improve accounting practices and make them more effective in the face of global problems. This is especially true of the cooperation between accounting and engineering, sociology, psychology, and information technologies. This cooperation can enable accountants to develop innovative solutions to global crises. To support this, accounting must focus on multidisciplinary approaches for the future.

An interdisciplinary approach requires the use and integration of methods and analytical frameworks from more than one academic discipline to examine a theme or topic. In the twenty-first century, accountants must adopt an interdisciplinary approach to the problems they have to solve. In other words, to use the digital systems correctly and effectively, accountants need to have knowledge and skills from different disciplines such as computer technology, programming language, statistics, and engineering.

Since the interdisciplinary approach uses multiple ideas and research methods, it can improve accounting practices and make them more effective in the face of global problems. It enables accountants to see the world as an integrated whole and learn how to solve a problem with knowledge gained from various disciplines.

The complex nature of the modern business environment and current research issues require scientists, accountants, and other professionals to work together. The interdisciplinary approach looks promising for opening new perspectives and encouraging more creative approaches to complex problems.

The essence of accounting is creative problem solving. It is essential to be able to predict the future more accurately. To do this, accountants will need knowledge other than taxation and technical information in the future.

The cooperation between accounting and engineering and information technologies can represent a reform movement to develop the skills and competencies to prepare accountants for life in the twenty-first century. These types of skills overlap with future competencies that accountants will need in the future, such as complex and creative problem solving, critical thinking, effective communication, and mathematical reasoning. This reform is an approach to answering questions, solving problems, and addressing contemporary economic issues by synthesizing knowledge from multiple disciplines.

An interdisciplinary approach helps with critical thinking and cognitive development of accountants. It enables them to improve themselves by establishing connections between ideas and concepts within different discipline boundaries. It can enrich the accounting profession through an emphasis on using multiple ideas and research methods. Let us suppose that you want to learn how digital systems work as a particular accountant. Therefore, you need to have some knowledge about computer technology, so you should become familiar with some aspects of computer science. You may need to use the science of statistics to analyze data in digital systems. For a complete understanding, you need to have skills from disciplines such as statistics, economics, foreign languages, and engineering.

IV.3-THE THEORY OF ACCOUNTING ENGINEERING

We can define digitalization in accounting as "**Digital Evolution**". Digital systems provided new materials, processes, and values for accountants to negotiate. As verbal culture gave way to digital and analytical culture, conventional practices began to be questioned.

As a focus of discussion, we can ask some questions such as "Will the accounting profession disappear?", "Will digital systems replace accountants?", and "How should we read digitalization in the accounting world"? Accounting engineering theory was born from these crucial questions. The necessity of building a brand-new language about digital systems became apparent in the processes of attempting to use digital systems correctly, accessing the right information, and managing it. Digital accounting involves much more than the ability to use a single digital system. The theory aims to discuss whether accounting engineering can be a new model for the accounting profession to adapt to the digital revolution, based on these questions. You can see the effects that the accounting engineering model will have on the accounting profession in Figure 7.

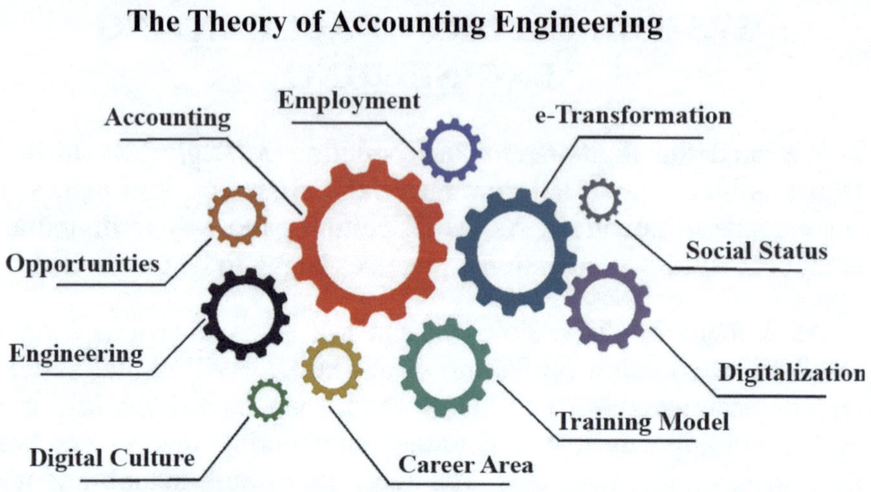

Figure 6. Graph of the Theory of Accounting Engineering

Accounting Engineering Theory: This course focuses on how accounting will be shaped on the basis of digitalization. It analyzes change and focuses on redesign.

Accounting engineering theory covers the concepts, principles, and procedures that form the basis of digitalization of accounting. It addresses the issue of how to shape accounting on this basis. The theory deals with the effects of digitization on the accounting structure and accountants, analyzes change and focuses on redesign. Design is an activity that is subject to rational scrutiny, but where creativity is also thought to play an important role.

Accounting engineering theory derives from systematic principles and methodology statements of accounting. It is the application of engineering principles and problem-solving techniques in the accounting field. The role of this theory is to improve accounting practices within the framework of digitalization and to solve the problems that will emerge with digitalization.

The purpose of the theory is to propose a new model of accounting. It does this by providing a consistent set of logical principles that constitute the general framework of reference for evaluating and improving the effects of digitalization on accounting practices.

It is not sufficient to change a single material, tool, or technique in pursuit of digital transformation; perceptions must be changed, too. Accounting education should be conducted in a way that improves these perceptions and awareness. The theory aims to reshape existing accounting education within the framework of engineering capabilities by predicting how the profession and its members will be affected by digitalization.

With digitization, members of the accounting profession will probably experience the following changes:

- Tendency to follow new technologies continuously,
- Decreasing emotion and action in accounting transactions, using reason with priority,
- Experiencing modern diseases such as anxiety, stress, and tension in the process of adapting to rapidly advancing technology with digitalization,
- Digitalization changing business habits, changing, and reshaping of the tools used in the execution of the profession,
- Emergence of training requirements to acquire technological skills,
- Differentiations in competencies and thinking styles with digital transformation.

Some questions about the effects of digitalization on the accounting profession:

- How will the accounting profession and members of the profession be affected by digitalization?
- How should we read digitalization in the accounting world?
- How can members of the accounting profession manage to stay up to date in the face of rapidly developing digitalization?
- What is the impact of digitalization on accounting education?

- How will the accounting profession take shape in the future with digitalization?
- Will the accounting profession disappear because of digitalization? Will digital systems replace the members of the accounting profession?

Principles of the Theory of Accounting Engineering

- It is based on the principle of rebuilding the accounting profession from A to Z in areas such as thought, education, technology, and culture with digitalization.
- It is a process that allows digitalization and the accounting profession to integrate with each other.
- It claims that accountants need basic engineering skills such as digital intelligence, effective communication, problem solving, analytical thinking, continuous learning, creativity, and looking at events from the big picture to use digital systems effectively and efficiently.
- The starting point of accounting engineering is being a member of the accounting profession. It keeps members of the accounting profession up to date in the digitalization cycle.
- Accounting engineering is the new career field for professional accountants.
- Accounting engineering aims to transform the accounting profession into a profession that creates added value and preserves business values by saving it from being a recording and reporting profession.

Digitalization and technological developments affect the accounting profession in strategic areas such as education, definition of accounting, the qualifications of members of the accounting profession, accounting practices, and thought and culture.

In order for the profession to keep up with the digital age, these areas must be redesigned. This can only be done through education reform, and the name of this education reform is accounting engineering. The accounting engineering department prepares candidates and members of the accounting profession for the future by helping them adapt in digital transformation in terms of culture, thought and competence. However, today's education is behind on technological developments and far from current digital thinking. Educational practices are based on knowledge and techniques from 10 to 15 years ago. For example, new accounting students are not given sufficient education regarding new digital systems. Recent research shows that current accountants are trying to learn these new digital systems through social media such as Youtube, Facebook or by trial-and-error method.

Education still covers conventional methods such as bookkeeping and tax statement submission. However, those conventional methods have been completely digitized. The duties of the members of the profession are now being transformed to include analysis, interpretation, and strategy. For this reason, education programs should be updated so as to provide future accountant candidates with these skills and competencies. At this stage, my recommendation is that the education reform should be made within the framework of engineering capabilities. It is not just about being a better accountant, it is also about better reading, being more educated and open-minded, being able to deal with different thoughts and building a broader set of skills.

With rapidly changing global scenarios and increasing competition, the accounting profession is faced with rapidly evolving technology and the need to develop customized solutions and complex models to solve difficult customer problems. The Covid-19 pandemic created brand new challenges for accountants, from solving complex incentive schemes to adapting to new technologies, to steering their customers to uncharted waters and to protecting their own businesses as well as their clients' businesses. All these have made it necessary to create a new discipline for the accounting profession.

Accounting engineering is the development and creative application of comprehensive, innovative accounting technologies; it is the art of finding better ways to address the needs of businesses and applying new technologies. It can also be key to dealing with global crises such as Covid-19. It can enable accountants to understand all aspects of innovation in the business world and turn it into practical solutions.

Accounting engineering uses information from the fields of information technology, statistics, economics, and applied mathematics, addresses current financial problems, and uses that knowledge to integrate new technologies into the accounting profession. Accounting engineering is technically and quantitatively based on conventional accounting disciplines. While conventional accounting uses traditional accounting information to record and report financial transactions of firms or individuals, accounting engineering creates advanced accounting applications by using advanced mathematics, programming, and algorithm information. Accounting engineering includes creativity as much as technical information. Because accounting engineering is an innovative and pioneering field, it is ever focused on management and innovation.

Thomas Kuhn opened a new era in the philosophy of science with his book The Structure of Scientific Revolutions, popularizing the widely discussed concept of "paradigm". According to Kuhn, while every new paradigm contributes to the development of knowledge, it does not invalidate previous knowledge. According to him, in a situation where "there is no particular paradigm or paradigm candidate", "it is not possible to distinguish the relative importance of all factors that may be distantly related to the development of a particular discipline".[52] Therefore, we can think of accounting engineering as a paradigmatic change that improves and transforms conventional accounting without neglecting it. In this context, it turns out that the change created by the digitalization of accounting requires a multidisciplinary approach through interdisciplinary integration. Accounting engineering is a new model created by conventional accounting applications and engineering applications such as advanced mathematics, algorithms, and artificial intelligence.

Accounting engineering can be implemented at universities in two programs: one for undergraduate education and one for graduate studies. Current members of the profession can study accounting

---

52 Omodeo, P. D. (2016). Kuhn's paradigm of paradigms: historical and epistemological coordinates of'The Copernican revolution'. In *Shifting paradigms: Thomas S. Kuhn and the history of science* (pp. 71-104). Edition Open Access.

engineering as a master's degree program. Accountant candidates, on the other hand, can study the undergraduate department of Accounting Engineering and graduate through a reshaped education process. For members of the accounting profession, learning what they will need tomorrow is as important as what they need to know today. For this reason, accounting engineering is a developing career field offering the learning skills and tasks necessary for members of the accounting profession to thrive in the digital age.

Why do Accounting Professionals Need Engineering Skills?

In conventional accounting education, there are few mathematics and numerical courses, and they are taught at the arithmetic four operations level. Problem solving, statistics, algorithms, and equation training are almost never included in the teaching program. However, digital transformation has made data meaningful by classifying and analyzing it with certain programming and algorithms, and data science has become more important. Therefore, members of the profession need these skills to accurately analyze and interpret digital data. Accountants need to understand how numbers work.

Accountants are not computer engineers. No one expects them to create digital systems, but they need to be able to monitor the functions and outputs of digital systems, as well as to understand them — to be able to change them — so that they can make better decisions.

We can define accounting engineering as bringing mathematical applications, system design, analytical thinking, engineering methods, technical tools, and case studies to the field of accounting.

In the engineering profession, when events are evaluated more broadly, then problems can be solved more easily. In business life, engineers are preferred for problem solving and numerical work. The best example of this is the banking sector. Engineers are hired in this sector because complex derivatives in banking include numerical questions and engineers have the ability to think fast and analytically to address these questions. For example, today's cancer research is done by software engineers, not by doctors. Engineers can actively use high-tech products and design flows and systems using them. The accounting engineering education program also aims to bring these competencies to the members of the profession.

Technology has the potential to commodify the basic services of the accounting profession and to radically reshape all roles of accountants. We can benefit from technology by applying a methodology that does not resist constant optimization and change in our workflow.

It is of critical importance to understand and adopt the technological developments for the future of the accounting profession. We have to know new technological tools such as artificial intelligence, blockchain, RSO, cloud systems and big data. Engineering gives us the capabilities we need to understand and use these technologies. Engineering knowledge is required to manage the continuous workflow optimization required by today's accounting practices and to analyze and interpret data in digital systems. For example, businesses need good quality data to perform complex tasks such as predicting accounting and finance trends. This is where accounting engineers come into play. Accounting engineers can collect, verify, analyze, interpret, and develop strategies for accounting information in a manner that businesses can use.

Presently, in the education given in universities and professional organizations, some efforts are made to adapt to digitalization. However, the current accounting education system is not enough to prepare accountants to work with technology. The accounting engineering education program can manage this process by directly using technologies in education. In summary, while the present education is trying to adapt to digitalization, accounting engineering aims to manage this process.

Conventional education is far from digital transformation culture and thought. Another objective of the accounting engineering education program is to bring this culture and idea to the members of the profession. The support of the members of the profession, international professional organizations and universities is very important in the implementation and legal framework of accounting engineering.

IV.4-THE CONCEPTUAL FRAMEWORK OF ACCOUNTING ENGINEERING AND THE RELATIONSHIP OF ACCOUNTING WITH ENGINEERING

Accounting engineering is the redesign of the accounting profession within the framework of engineering abilities in the light of technological developments such as digitalization, artificial intelligence, and the 4th Industrial Revolution to prepare the accounting profession for the future. Accounting engineering makes use of tools such as applied mathematics, computer science, software, statistics, and economic theory in this process. Accounting engineering is a multidisciplinary field that includes engineering methods, mathematical tools, and programming practice. The accounting engineer acts as an interface between conventional engineering disciplines and accounting systems and can work in both directions – by applying engineering design or generating new approaches to accounting practice. Accounting engineers will also encourage innovation in the accounting profession.

There will be two types of people in the new accounting world; those who are interested in running the business and those who are interested in making further changes. To fulfill the promise of the future business model, it will not be sufficient for the members of the accounting profession to solve different accounting problems, they will also have to put aside conventional accounting ideas. Accountants will need the right skills to enable businesses to use technology effectively. Perhaps the most important step for the members of the accounting profession is to focus on improving their business acumen.

Definition of Accounting Engineering and Its Necessity

Conventional accounting was defined as the discipline that records, classifies, summarizes, analyzes the events expressed monetarily, and presents them to information users through commenting. This definition has transformed the members of the profession into a profile type that only makes records and tries to carry out their profession with tax awareness. The biggest concern of the members of the profession has been to make statements and declarations requested by public institutions within the legal period. However, developments have brought us the questions of how the accounting profession can be managed and what skills are required for the future. In the twenty-first century, it has become imperative for professionals to plan their own path and define the future of the profession.

With the impact of big data, the members of the profession turned towards providing more benefits to information users by engaging in data and analysis instead of recording, classifying, and summarizing data. In the future stocks, machines, and other assets will be in communication with each other with smart accounting systems. In the process of Industry 4.0, machines will not only produce products, but stocks will be able to communicate with the machines and transfer data to them about what to do. Even this situation gives us a new perspective on where the accounting profession is headed. In the near future, the recording, classification, and summarizing tasks that are included in the accounting definition and constitute its basic functions will be carried out by these smart systems.

Data-intensive tasks will be organized by automation systems in the future. Big data may inevitably change the role of the accountants, but I am one of those who think the human touch will still be needed. I think we will continue to need unique human qualities such as leadership, empathy, creativity, and intuition.

In the future, virtual accountants will be able to perform guidance and auditing by making intervention in smart production systems without going to the workplace. The professional accountants of the future should be persons who can solve possible errors in the system with proactive approaches with an analytical mind and critical thinking skills.

Engineering is an applied branch; it is a pioneering profession that designs physical components required to make people's lives easier, it ensures the production, continuity, and availability of these components in the society, and it contributes to technological and economic development.

Modern accountants need to be familiar with normative science questions in order to utilize the potential of accounting and to create a sustainable foundation for green technology.

The engineering approach is a good methodology for framing and solving multifaceted digital transformation problems. Engineering offers a unique opportunity to integrate emerging technological developments into accounting practices.

Accounting engineering is concerned with "financial transactions and decisions that belong to the accounting profession, made by members of the accounting profession and businesses". According to this approach, accounting engineering is a profession and an interdisciplinary approach. It works to solve the problems encountered in accounting by using the analytical experience of engineering and it aims to achieve progress in the field of technological development.

To determine the role that accounting engineering can play in accounting science, it is necessary to examine the basic philosophy of science. The main concern of this approach is that the conventional structure of the accounting profession tends to ignore the problems and decisions regarding the impact of technology on accounting. Because technological risks are one of the sources of concern in a conventional structure. Technological risks bring about issues such as the disappearance of the accounting profession in the future. On the other hand, the redesign of the accounting profession will draw more attention to issues such as digitalization and sustainability. The redesign of the accounting profession is a response to social and technological developments.

Since it is based on systematic thinking and the ability for mathematical thinking, engineering synthesizes all the knowledge obtained through science through reason and experience and generates formations that are beneficial to humanity. The field of engineering strives to find the most ideal solution by making the best use of science, economy, time, and physical resources. Engineers, who can produce new ideas for industry and technologies, can also guide existing thoughts and change the living conditions of humanity with their decisions. The analytical skills of engineering enable accountants to concentrate on accounting practices and analyze huge data sets. In the light of these explanations, we can define accounting engineering as follows: "Accounting engineers are people who have the skills to design systems in line with technological developments, analyze and interpret digital and big data correctly, define accounting problems and produce scientific solutions to these problems, and who redesign the financial structure and future of enterprises and develop new strategies."

An accounting engineer does not need to have an engineering background or know how to write code. What is essential is that the accounting engineers must think like engineers. What makes people "successful product managers" at Google is their engineering talent. Because engineering skills include a good grasp of algorithms and the ability to manage them.

When you examine all the technologies that shape the future of the accounting profession, you can see that they have been created by engineers. However, accountants are also an important part of this process. Because accountants have the best knowledge of the fine points and details in the accounting profession. For example, if you are creating an accounting algorithm, you will need an accountant to design the system correctly. Consider a business model that has both accounting and engineering skills at the same time. Believe me, this may make the future much simpler and more understandable for accounting.

Accounting engineers are people who have specialized in their field, combining their theoretical and practical knowledge with philosophy, mathematics, and other branches of science in parallel with technological developments.

"Accounting engineering" is a visionary term for the contemporary accounting profession that includes engineering skills and twenty-first century technologies. This revolution is a set of values consisting of analysis, strategy, interpretation, data science, creativity, design, engineering, information technologies and information systems. This concept makes the accounting profession more efficient, as it will transform the accounting profession from verbal culture to analytical and digital culture as a result of engineering skills. Accounting urgently needs analytical thinkers who can solve digital transformation problems. We need engineering skills to educate this type of accountant thinkers.

The Relationship between Accounting and Engineering

A new approach to interdisciplinary work is essential to realize the digital transformation of accounting. The basis of accounting and engineering comprises collecting information, analyzing, and interpreting it, developing solutions, and reporting these solutions and outputs for decision makers. Both branches of science are data-driven and move with input-process-output stages.

Engineering and accounting branches have become more closely related recently and a symbiotic relationship has emerged between them. Modern social sciences are among the most important branches of accounting and engineering sciences. Apart from that, considering the extraordinary nature and scale of the accounting problems we face today, collaborations with disciplines, where we can combine our talents in both quantitative and qualitative fields, will add value to the accounting profession. Bringing the two disciplines together will both create a better understanding and also enable better use of accounting to improve the economic level of businesses.

The concept of accounting engineering is based on the collaboration between accounting and engineering skill sets. Engineering is a science branch that will succeed in understanding the conventional and variable structure of accounting while integrating it into technological advancements. More specifically, we can make use of engineering science to achieve the digital transformation of the accounting profession. This is where accounting engineering comes in and aims to redesign the accounting profession based on engineering and analytical thinking capability.

Accounting engineering is a field that is open to development while located at the intersection of mathematics and accounting. It makes use of the fields of computer science, numerical methods, economics, mathematics, and linear algebra equations. With so many different engineering disciplines today, it is not surprising that engineering is in almost every aspect of our lives. Also, many accounting managers have also chosen to obtain an engineering degree.

The Future of Jobs report, prepared by the World Economic Forum every two years, lists the skills that will be most needed by 2025[53]. According to the report, these skills are as follows:

- Analytical thinking and innovation
- Active learning and learning strategies
- Complex problem solving
- Critical thinking and analysis
- Creativity, originality, and initiative
- Leadership and social influence
- Technology use, monitoring and control
- Technology design and programming
- Resilience, stress tolerance and flexibility
- Reasoning, problem solving and ideation
- Emotional intelligence
- Troubleshooting and user experience
- Service orientation
- System analysis and evaluation
- Persuasion and negotiation

We can say that the competencies and qualifications that accounting engineering will bring to the accountants are compatible with these skills.

One of the effects of engineering on the accounting profession is the scientific management approach, which is a theory that analyzes and synthesizes workflows. Scientific management is the application of scientific techniques to problems and difficulties. Using scientific methods in accounting operations will increase efficiency and speed. The combination of disciplines that are of critical importance for both facing global challenges and foreseeing a new future in the name of accounting will train accountants who can make analysis using

53 http://www3.weforum.org/docs/WEF_Future_of_Jobs_2020.pdf

various methods in all kinds of information systems, focus on design as a whole, and thereby improve accounting as a whole.

We can list the abilities that accounting engineering will develop in members of the accounting profession as follows:

- The ability to question that will be used to make abstractions that guide thoughts, instead of thinking based on a certain pattern,
- Abstraction and analytical expression ability,
- Ability to apply the concepts of "optimization, probability and statistics" in the decision-making process,
- To have a command of both accounting and engineering fields,
- Analytical and numerical thinking, effective communication, problem solving and creativity ability,
- Ability to have a holistic view of the events concerning accounting,
- Ability to convey ideas to others and persuade people,
- Ability to see into the future and perceive opportunities,
- High success motivation and creativity, featured work,
- Ability to make good use of time and perform teamwork.

Engineering is the most practical of the disciplines. It has a special position against many other sciences. It is based on fundamental principles that develop mindsets and analyze problems analytically to their core. In recent years, different fields of information have expanded enormously in both quantity and quality: As new disciplines emerge, conventional disciplines have expanded their knowledge base enormously. Skills such as mathematics, logic, analysis, scientific reasoning, and rational thinking are indisputable for engineers. Accounting engineering is the process of reform of the accounting profession within the framework of these engineering capabilities. It aims to integrate accounting with skills that encourage logic, synthesis, mathematics, intuition, critical thinking, and creative problem solving.

IV.5-THE CONCEPTUAL EXISTENCE REASON OF ACCOUNTING ENGINEERING

There are two questions that accountants could be curious about: "Does the accountancy profession really need a re-design for digital transformation?" and "Can't the transformation be achieved with current and conventional methods?" I believe the accounting profession needs a radical change to become more innovative. Digital transformation represents a break from the past. Change is essential if we want to ensure the success of the accounting profession in the future. For this reason, we must focus on the needs and requirements of digital transformation. What we need is a profound redesign, which is the driving force behind transformation and evolution. If we are to implement a successful digital transformation strategy, adopting a new framework of design-oriented thinking is the right method. Because design is the key to solving problems and discovering opportunities for digital transformation.

It is particularly important to understand the needs of transformation for digital innovations to happen. This is exactly where design thinking is best used. Design-oriented thinking is an approach used to solve problems and explore opportunities for digital transformation. In recent years, design has evolved into more than just replacing objects. It has been transformed into an approach to rebuild logic, imagination, empathy, and business models.

Defining the concept of the problem is the first and most important step in design thinking. Not only does this help us seize the opportunity, but it also helps us review the opportunity before we start creating solutions. Empathize, define, design, model, test. These are the five steps that make up the design thinking.

Design-oriented thinking is a tool that helps to better conceptualize the tasks. It allows us to understand new business processes and to make a measurable assessment as we approach a large project. This way, we question the scope and narrowness of our thought process and push our boundaries. Design-oriented thinking is the key to transforming business models and the foundation for creating digital transformation strategies. Design-oriented thinking is actively used by innovative companies such as Google and Amazon.

Change is indispensable if we want to ensure the success of the accounting profession in the future. For Deloitte, the right response is "not to squeeze creative talent and customers in a zero-sum battle to capture more of the existing pie [but rather] to discover new ways of organizing and operating to more effectively create and capture new value" Innovators do not target disproportionally high salaries of creative workers to encourage change. Rather, they recommend that corporate managers organize new and efficient ways of valorizing the human workforce.

Digital transformation is a revolution for business models in all aspects. The power behind it is technology. It offers two options for businesses and industries: adapting or falling behind. Our duty is to use the magic of design to realize the digital transformation of the accounting profession.

An accounting engineer must be curious and open to innovation. He does not need to be an advanced speaker but must be capable of communicating his thoughts clearly. The universal language of accounting engineering is English. An accounting engineer must have the necessary English speaking and writing skills. The accounting engineer also needs to have a certain amount of programming skills. In addition, he should have knowledge about linear algebra, stochastic analyses, spatial geometry, and differential equations. Mathematics is part of the accounting engineering curriculum, and it is necessary to have expertise in this area, as it will be used frequently in simulated accounting cases. An accounting engineer needs to keep up with the latest market trends.

We can list the basic features of accounting engineers as follows:

- The purpose of an accounting engineer, beyond bookkeeping, statement preparation, tax services and preparing financial statements, is to design financial statements, to analyze them, to interpret the tables, to define financial problems, to produce fast, efficient, economical and standard solutions to these problems within the framework of scientific and mathematical principles, to build the financial structure and future of companies, to develop strategies in this direction and to implement these strategies.

• An accounting engineer thinks positively, is self-confident, decisive, produces solutions, thinks in corporate terms, takes risks, is impartial, modest, fair, and balanced, sociable, human-oriented, has analytical thinking skills and theoretical and practical knowledge to be able to make designs.

• They think statistically. They are professionals who convert digital data into information.

• They make use of scientific principles in their work.

• They have the ability to collect, analyze and interpret digital data.

• They are strategy experts. They make predictions about the financial structure and future of the business.

• Their main purpose is to ensure the existence and continuity of the business.

• They make use not only of accounting science, but also other branches of science in their work.

• They have innovative ideas about the future.

• The foundation of his work is based on designing and building the financial structure by using the resources of the businesses in the best way.

Today, the most advanced countries in the world in terms of innovation owe their success to integrating the design-oriented thinking method into their education systems and institutions. The best companies in the world such as Apple, Facebook and Google did not come into being by themselves. They are the products of creativity and design-oriented thinking. Engineering and design-oriented thinking can offer us the digital accounting of the future.

IV.6- THE EDUCATIONAL PROCESSES OF ACCOUNTING ENGINEERING

The scope of teaching and learning has changed in the last two decades. With the emergence of new technologies, unlimited access to knowledge and information has changed the nature of education. Assessing the value of conventional methods has become critical. Along with academicians and decision makers, some research also calls for change in teaching methods.

The scope and agenda of accounting education largely depends on how technology evolves. The first half of the twentieth century is based on conventional accounting practices in terms of both cultural and economic approaches. The second half of the twentieth century, on the other hand, witnessed a more technological and diverse accounting that went beyond conceptualization as a historical necessity. Accounting education in the twenty-first century should not be about conventional accounting practices but should include the technological development process.

In the world, accounting education is evolving in a direction supported by digital media and tools. It has become impossible to design the cornerstones of education such as pedagogy, learning, measurement, and evaluation, learning outcomes without including the effects of technology. Methods and theories of accounting are taking shape in a technology-centered manner. Conventional accounting methods have lost their effectiveness in today's accounting education. To keep up with the advancing technology and educate a digital generation, it is important to use this technology by integrating it with new teaching methods. Important and radical change for the accounting profession is approaching. This offers us a great opportunity to make the profession more strategic and reliable than ever before. This award requires us to embrace change and educate and develop people with different skills and abilities.

An old proverb says, "The best time to plant a tree was 20 years ago. The second-best time is now." Now is the best time to act if we want success in the future. For the digital transformation of accounting, education reform must be the first issue to address and today is the best time to begin.

ACCA defines seven constituent areas for the members of the accounting to be successful in the future:[54]

1. **Technical skills and ethics:** The skills and abilities to perform activities consistently to a defined standard while maintaining the highest standards of integrity, independence, and skepticism.

2. **Communication skills**: The ability to acquire and use knowledge: thinking, reasoning, and solving problems.

3. **Creativity**: The ability to use existing knowledge in a new situation, to make connections, explore potential outcomes and generate new ideas.

4. **Digital**: The awareness and application of existing and emerging digital technologies, capabilities, practices, and strategies.

5. **Emotional intelligence**: The ability to identify your own emotions and those of others, harness and apply them to tasks, and regulate and manage them.

6. **Vision**: The ability to anticipate future trends accurately by extrapolating existing trends and facts, and filling the gaps by thinking innovatively

7. **Experience:** The ability and skills to understand customer expectations, meet desired outcomes and create value.

The quality of education of accountants directly affects the accounting practices and the management process of businesses. For this reason, accountants are expected not only to generate information or data, but also to be able to analyze and interpret them, and especially to use them in decision-making processes. In other words, accountants are expected to be people who guide businesses in all

54 https://www.accaglobal.com/gb/en/qualifications/why-acca/competency-framework/quotients.html

accounting affairs, be skilled in human relations and knowledgeable about human psychology, fluent in foreign languages, follow domestic and international developments, be aware of economic and political events, develop strategies to achieve business goals, update and educate themselves. Accounting engineers must have the character to manage all processes affecting accounting such as finance, tax, economy, and information technologies. At the present, accounting students are learning IT skills at work on their own or with the help of some professional training offered by employers.

Conventional accounting training does not have the structure which can respond to globalization, digitalization, technological developments, and corporate governance practices. The accounting engineering education process should be designed to respond to today's circumstances and individuals should be given the ability to question by developing critical thinking.

In the twenty-first century accounting is driven by globalization, international standards, legal changes, developments in information and communication technologies, economic developments, and new management approaches in businesses and economic changes. Within the framework of these changes, education can be restructured as follows:

- The ıdea that the accounting system only consists of bookkeeping or tax work should be abandoned. When the accounting system updates itself, this progress should not remain within the accounting system only; this update should cover the fields of economy, finance, law, and business administration. In addition to accounting information, accounting education should be integrated with other fields, accountants should be given the opportunity to interpret and analyze the information they gained and use it in decision-making processes. Accounting curricula should include general education courses such as economy, law, finance, business administration, mathematics, philosophy, information technology, literature, music, and theater as well as accounting. This will not only enable individuals with accounting education to use their accounting learning in an integrated manner, but it also enables businesses to use their knowledge and skills to keep up with modern times.

• Global accounting education is of great importance in the education of accountants who can access information in the fastest way, make use of their knowledge in production processes, adapt to the changing conditions of the modern age, are not afraid of taking risks, do not hesitate to take part in decision-making processes, can be a part of the solution instead of a problem, do not hesitate to question and express their thoughts, and have advanced listening skills.

• Science and technology are in interaction with the field of economy, and developments in economy also affect the science of accounting. As a result of this, individuals who provide accounting education should follow the developments in the field of economy and be aware of the reflections of these developments in the field of accounting. Lecturers working in the departments of universities related to accounting should prevent accounting from getting stuck in theory and harmonize accounting with current economic developments. Accounting education, which is not associated with current events, does not attract the attention of accounting students, and prevents them from being sufficiently informed when they enter business life.

• Accounting education institutions cannot train graduates with the skills demanded by the business world without incorporating current and developing information technologies into accounting education and adding various IT-based accounting practices and technologies to their curriculum.

• In this educational model, it is particularly important to teach accounting students skills such as advanced computer and internet use, accounting software, technology security and controls.

• Information technology competencies are one of the basic technical skills that accounting graduates should have. Universities must include software programs and applications such as network security, IT controls, ERP, business intelligence and strategic corporate management into their curricula to educate the accounting graduates of the future. On a pedagogical level, incorporating IT-related topics into key accounting technical issues will provide contextual understanding and deep learning.

• Philosophy directs people to thinking and research. Philosophy and psychology should also be included in accounting education for the development of accountants who think, research and question.

- Accounting solves the problems of businesses. For this reason, educational processes should be multidimensional and dynamic to include comprehensive knowledge about human emotions, thoughts, and behaviors, and use this information in problem solving.

- Courses such as advanced mathematics, which cover engineering skills, sociology, foreign language, econometrics, critical thinking, accounting technologies should be taught in accounting education.

Today, it is not enough to graduate from universities with a basic accounting qualification. Accounting education needs to be redesigned from A-to-Z to meet all the requirements of the twenty-first century. The verbal-based education system should be transformed into a system which offers numerical, analytical, and data-based education. However, both public institutions and the private sector should fulfill their responsibilities in accounting education, engage in dialogue with each other, and carry out joint research and projects.

The accounting engineering program should offer bachelor's and master's degrees by being integrated with digital applications, as well as the disciplines of information science, management science, econometrics, advanced mathematics, philosophy, and sociology. The graduate level is a program designed to transform members of the accounting profession who have graduated from the conventional accounting education program, and the undergraduate level is a program designed for accountant candidates within the framework of current and global conditions. The program should be conducted in English; its distinctive feature from other programs is that it is based on mathematics and information technologies. Case studies and computer modeling exercises will teach students how to apply techniques to real data.

The accounting engineering department works on engineering and accounting interfaces to develop accounting practices and generate solutions to problems. It prepares its students to be leaders in academia and industry. Its education reflects the interdisciplinary nature of accounting engineering and includes homework. This department is designed to educate accounting engineers who can design systems, analyze, and interpret digital and big data accurately, define accounting problems, produce solutions to these problems that are efficient, economic, and compliant with standards within the framework of scientific and mathematical principles, build the accounting structure and future of enterprises, develop, and implement strategies.

The accounting engineering department develops specialized skills in accounting and engineering and aims to educate accountants with deep thinking and comprehensive decision-making skills, along with basic academic skills to deeply understand the future of accounting.

One of the objectives of the accounting engineering program is to provide members of accounting professionals with digital accounting literacy. For this reason, the digital systems of the Ministry of Finance should be included in the courses comprehensively.

The objective of designing this department is to ensure that members of the accounting profession can take part in senior executive positions who provide guidance to businesses in business life, build their financial structures, make decisions, manage economic crises, and develop strategies. Accounting engineers will be trained to foresee accounting errors and create safe accounting designs that protect against unforeseen problems. The accounting engineering program includes problem solving, data reliance, dimensional analysis and logic-chain based basic skill sets.

The accounting engineering program should provide an educational process in accordance with international standards within the framework of globalization, international standards and legal changes, developments in information and communication technologies, economic developments, corporate management in enterprises and economic crises. A rich and comprehensive curriculum should be prepared with courses such as econometrics, philosophy of technology, advanced mathematics, sociology, critical thinking, coding languages, psychology, foreign language, risk management, mathematical modeling, accounting engineering and digital transformation, decision analysis, strategic thinking, and accounting technologies, which are not taught comprehensively in today's accounting education.

The objective of the accounting engineering education program is to train accountants who follow technological and scientific developments, combine theoretical and practical knowledge with mathematics and science, follow global developments, have a competent, productive, participatory, critical thinking capability, can learn on their own over their whole life, can take responsibility, can produce in the international arena, and can comply with ethical values.

Accounting engineering program aims to train professional accountants who can use and manage digital systems, build mathematical models, and solve them with calculation methods, and have a strong technical background in the field of information systems.

The skills that an accounting engineer should have can be listed as follows:

- Self-Learning and Lifelong Learning Skills.
- Problem Solving, Creative Thinking and Criticism Skills.
- Technical and Social Communication Skills.
- Self-Assessment Skills.
- Deductive Reasoning - The ability to apply general rules to specific problems to generate logical answers.
- Inductive Reasoning - The ability to combine bits of information to form general rules or conclusions (involves finding a relationship between seemingly unrelated events).
- Mathematics - Knowledge of arithmetic, algebra, geometry, calculus, statistics, and their applications.
- Science - Using scientific rules and methods to solve problems.
- Using Mathematics to Solve Problems and Mathematical Reasoning.
- Problem Responsiveness - The ability to say something is wrong or possibly will go wrong. It involves not solving the problem, but

simply admitting it is a problem.

• Analyzing Data or Information - Identifying the underlying principles, causes, or facts of the information by breaking down information or data into separate parts.

• Identifying Objects, Actions, and Events - Identifying information by categorizing, predicting, recognizing differences or similarities, and detecting changes in conditions or events.

• Creative Thinking - Developing, designing, or creating new applications, ideas, relationships, systems, or products, including artistic contributions.

• Analytical Thinking – This requires analyzing information and using logic to address business problems and issues.

• Skills to Improve Organizational Processes.

• Skills to Evaluate the Opportunities Arising from Technological Innovations.

• Skills to Design and Manage System and Accounting Structure.

• Skills to Identify and Evaluate Alternative Solutions and Methods

IV.7-THE EFFECTS OF ACCOUNTING ENGINEERING ON THE ACCOUNTING PROFESSION AND ECONOMIC LIFE

Professional problems experienced by accountants are discussed in the academic environment. Digitalization has made the conventional problems of the profession less important. Accounting engineering will provide benefits for both the profession's adaptation to technology and digitalization, and the solution of conventional problems.

Accounting engineering will improve qualifications of accountants, this, in turn, will improve salaries and benefits. With scientific thinking and engineering skill, accountants can produce efficient, economical, and effective solutions to problems within the framework of scientific principles. Accounting engineering prevents unnecessary competition by creating employment opportunities. It gives accountants the ability to solve problems, think creatively, and criticize. It places accountants at strategic positions in businesses and ensures that they take active roles in the development of business activities and achieving their goals. It provides home-office work opportunities in the accounting profession.

Globalization forces businesses to compete not only in the country but also in the international arena. To adapt to this and continue their existence, businesses need to change their management understanding in accordance with the competitive environment. Accounting engineers can contribute to the transformation of businesses with the good training they will receive. They can identify risks and problems that affect the business activities and produce solutions that eliminate them to use business resources effectively. Accounting engineers can make significant contributions to businesses for achieving their strategic goals. They can give the necessary responses in a timely manner to the normative, conscious, and regulatory pressures arising from the environment for businesses to have a long operational life. Accounting engineers are people who provide guidance to business owners and managers in building these processes and developing strategies. They have a solid grasp of accounting methods, technology expertise, business acumen and engineering skills.

Accounting engineers are people who can steer the businesses in accounting issues within the framework of these duties, are skilled in human relations and knowledgeable about human psychology, speak foreign languages, follow domestic and international developments frequently, are aware of economic and political events, and constantly update and educate themselves. They use mathematical formulas and engineering methods instead of conventional accounting practices. They are open minded and curious. They spend their time solving accounting problems. Accounting engineers have a high level of academic ability, the ability to think numerically, the power to convey ideas to others and persuade people, the ability to foresee and perceive opportunities, and the ability to make appropriate decisions and plans.

Accounting engineers are always informed about the latest accounting trends, emerging technologies, and current industry news. This enables accounting engineers not only to keep their jobs but also to provide more efficient services to their clients.

According to the research on "**Family Companies: Change and Continuity**", 65-80% of the businesses in the world are family businesses. As stated in the rest of the report, the average life expectancy of family businesses is 24 years, and seven tenths of family businesses do not pass on to the second generation. In other words, only three out of ten family companies are transferred to the second generation. About half of them disappear before the third generation. These companies are the foundation of the world economy, and they generate most of the employment, added value and production. Unfortunately, only 30 percent of these companies pass to the second generation.[55]

The reasons for the bankruptcy of companies were also mentioned in the report. The main reasons are the failure of enterprises to develop new products and business models and lack of capital. In addition to this, inability to think strategically, poor management, failure to institutionalize, failure to provide information flow, failure

---

55 Yolac, S., & Dogan, E. (2011). Kuresellesme Surecinde Aile Isletmelerinde Yonetim ve Kurumsallasma. *Istanbul Universitesi Iktisat Fakultesi Mecmuasi*, *61*(2), 83-110.

to control costs, failure to observe and predict changes in the markets, inadequate reporting in the company and inability to ask for a call to account are other reasons. In other words, family businesses are managed by business owners using unprofessional methods, and 85 percent of them cannot see the third generation because they cannot institutionalize.

Business managers have to make instant decisions due to the dizzying speed of modern business life. This situation comes back to accounting and finance managers in the form of additional pressure on their quality and time. Managers are now required to not only produce the right data, but also to do it in a short time. The capability to access information on time and use it properly provides companies with great competitive advantages. Unfortunately, accountants are still dealing with bookkeeping and tax services jobs that should be in the automation system. Here, the accounting engineering model is a model that will extend the life of family companies, institutionalize them, and create new business areas by responding to these needs of businesses.

One challenge the accounting profession is facing is permanence. To achieve this, it must integrate itself with other science branches such as engineering, philosophy, and advanced mathematics.

Let us not forget that right thinking comes before right action. Beyond brilliant technology and cool gadgets, digital transformation is fundamentally a philosophy of change to improve the lives of people. Creation and innovative processes are integral parts of this transformation. Digital transformation has the power to drastically change the entire process of a business model. Technology and new digital capabilities enable accountants to access data that was previously impossible to access, allowing them to perform financial tests at a speed that was impossible to achieve before.

For this reason, digital transformation requires more than technological innovations for the accounting profession. The digital transformation that radically changes all the building blocks of the accounting profession, opens the door to the question whether the title of "accountant", which is integrated with bookkeeping and tax services, is the right title for the accountants of the future.

The technologies of the twenty-first century will carry accounting professionals far beyond the title of "accountant" for both the society we live in and for the businesses. I hope the accounting engineering model will be implemented successfully and win through in the end. I hope that in this way, it will carry all accounting professionals into the future of accounting.

CHAPTER V
SPACE ACCOUNTING

From the ancient Mayan astronomy to Galileo, humanity's interest in space has remained alive throughout history. The idea of going to space is as old as human history. The desire of humans to live on other planets has been taken as a realistic idea by physicists. At the beginning of the twentieth-first century, technology reached a level where interplanetary space travel by humans could be realized.

Some space researchers claim that space flight could become part of our daily travels around the planet in the next fifty years. The space industry is composed of many moving parts. Consider all of the expenditures in the development and utilization phases of all its related products and services. They span from research and development within the scope of space exploration to the areas involving infrastructure, ground stations, launch vehicles and satellites.

Space industry is a fast-growing sector of the high-tech market. The global space economy was worth 423 billion dollars in 2019, and this amount will increase significantly with space mining and space tourism. According to the estimates of economists interested in the space market, the size of the space economy could increase to 2.5 to 3 trillion dollars in the next three years. Of course, there is a need for professional accounting at the intersection of all these economic developments and currency exchanges.

So, how will space exploration affect the accounting profession? Will we be able to solve accounting problems in space with conventional accounting methods?

It is presumed that today's accounting systems, based on recording and reporting, will be insufficient for the analysis of the big data resulting from all these economic activities in the space industry. This is because conventional accounting practices do not include any accounting practices and standards for economic activities in space. For this reason, it can be said that there is a need for an international accounting expertise that embraces new measurement units to determine the accounting practices and valuation methods for the relevant economic activities, to ensure transparency and uniformity in the accounting and recording system, to determine the principles, procedures, and basis for the proper and to ensure reliable accounting of activities in accordance with their true nature. In this context, the issue of "space accounting" is worth discussing as a field that needs new accounting expertise.

Space Economy

Resources on earth are limited. This limitation has become a defining feature of human existence, and the fact that supply is limited while demand is unlimited affects economies by driving up the costs of resources. However, this situation may change, thanks to developments in "space mining", a concept which came to the agenda in the early 1990s.

Space mining can be defined as the process of extracting rare and precious metals from small planets close to Earth. Celestial bodies such as asteroids contain metals such as platinum, iron, gold, and diamonds that are presently found on Earth. It is estimated that some asteroids contain a greater amount of platinum than has ever been obtained in the history of the Earth. In addition, space mining covers such works and activities as supplying mineral and gas from asteroids, iron, nickel, and titanium for use in structures to be built in space, water, and oxygen necessary for astronauts to continue their work in these structures, hydrogen, and oxygen for use as rocket fuel. These activities in space exploration are called "sourcing in place".

To date, 9000 asteroids have been discovered to be orbiting Earth. About 1,000 new asteroids are discovered every year. Studies show that an asteroid with a diameter of one kilometer contains 7,500 tons of precious metals worth over 150 billion dollars.

It is estimated that there are 12 thousand asteroids close to the Earth. Ten percent of these would be easier to reach, comparatively, than missions to reach the Moon. Some asteroids are estimated to contain enough iron, nickel, or cobalt to meet the world's needs for 3,000 years. They also have water in the form of water ice that can be used and transported in rocket fuels. Today, developed countries and commercial organizations are planning to extract these resources for profit and establish human colonies on Mars. In addition, some entrepreneurs state that asteroid mining can help to eliminate scarcity of some of these resources.

In addition to space exploration, the use of resources from other planets, asteroids, and similar bodies in space will be considered the first mining activity to take place in space – outside of planet Earth.

Works in the field of space tourism show that space may soon become an option as a holiday destination. Space tourism has a long history. The Russian Space Agency can be considered the first company to successfully carry out orbital space tourism. In the early 2000s, seven people were sent to space as space tourists.

The popularity of the idea of space tourism is increasing day by day. This has increased the number of businesses participating in tourism activities in the space industry. Some of these companies are Richard Branson's Virgin Galactic company, SpaceX company founded by Elon Musk, co-founder of Tesla electric car company, and Blue Origin company owned by Jeff Bezos, founder of Amazon. This rapid increase in the quality of the economic values in the space industry requires many different specialties that can manage the economic activities in space accurately and effectively. Accounting information systems also need to pay more attention to space exploration; because the actual direction of space exploration is also influenced by the accounting profession, although it was initially developed in relation to sciences such as engineering, mathematics, and physics.

These economic activities also necessitate the development of a new accounting system and language. Because a new accounting approach and/or expertise will be needed in order to manage space tourism and mining correctly, to make sound analyses and interpretations, and to make the right decisions.

Transformation of Accounting into Space Dimension

Accounting is a set of assumptions, frameworks and methodologies used in the examination and application of financial reporting principles. It is a constantly evolving subject and must adapt to new ways of doing business, new technological standards and gaps discovered in reporting mechanisms. Today, the space economy is proposed as a new field of study comparable to other fields such as the agricultural economy, the maritime economy, and the industrial economy. As in other fields of study, we need to negotiate on a new conceptual framework to determine the principles, procedures, and basis for determining the accounting application and valuation methods for economic activities in space, ensuring transparency and uniformity in the accounting and recording system, and determining the accurate and reliable accounting of the activities in accordance with their true nature. As space exploration advances, especially in areas such as asteroid mining, space tourism, and space production, questions facing the accounting field emerge in a much clearer manner. In this context, we need an in-depth study examining the scientific and technological effects of space research in terms of accounting, which affect the conventional structure of accounting. Key issues concerning the problems that may arise in accounting science with space economy and space exploration are given in Figure

Figure 7. Key issues in the science of accounting that may arise with space discoveries

One of the most dynamic and controversial challenges of this century in accounting will probably be the search for accounting standards in the face of economic events in space.

Will accounting work differently when it goes off the Earth? Of course not. However, when we leave the boundaries of the Earth, we need to think about basic assumptions such as how financial reporting will be done, which accounting measurements and valuation methods will be used, and in which currency the financial statements will be presented. Especially with space production, we must be ready to answer the fundamental questions that will arise about new costing models, reporting standards and new skills that accountants need to acquire. Because this situation is important for sustainable space activities.

The transformation of accounting into the dimension of off-planet space should include not only technical accounting and financial reporting, but also issues related to business processes and auditing. Legal and regulatory frameworks, technology infrastructure, as well as tax and contracts, compensation and human resources are the primary conceptual issues. Strictly speaking, this transformation requires more than changing the chart of accounts and accounting standards.

Accounting will need to report the specified space activities accurately and on time in accordance with the needs of all stakeholders of the space industry. Governments will be concerned with taxes, employees with wages, partners with profits, customers with the quality of service, suppliers with assurance of their receivables, and banks with the return of their loans. So, who will be in charge of taxation? Will government agencies or associations yet to be formed be authorized to collect the tax? How will the ownership of earnings be determined? Will the scope of taxation be determined with prevention of double taxation agreements and/or similar agreements, or will it be necessary to exempt it from tax by saying "this issue creates an alternative to the consumption of the world's scarce resources?" Or, maybe the priority will be to protect the world global economy with taxes or tariffs as if it were a common market with a single customs wall against space resources. So how will the earnings and taxation base be determined? Will this issue be solved with existing tax laws or with brand new tax practices specific to space? Will this sector have measurement and value units specific to it or even its own new monetary unit in the form of space currency? With these questions that begin to come to mind, we are taking a philosophical journey from the unknown to the unknown. First, we must create a discussion ground about space accounting that is based on reasonable thought.

At the center of all these discussions, there is strong suspicion that the accounting, auditing, and reporting standards in practice today will not be sufficient for accurate and requirement-oriented reporting of the new economic activities that are imagined to be possible with the near future normalization of space industry.

If we consider these new economic activities and space industry concepts, we can imagine there will be a demand for the activation of vehicles that will transport passengers to space, there will need to be construction, activation, and a cost determination of living spaces to be established on any planet or star, hotels to be accommodated, and satellite stations to be fueled in space. In this context, space accounting will ensure that the commercial activities of organizations working in the field of space exploration are reflected in the financial statements in the same way, that financial statements can be understood in the same way, similar events will be interpreted in a similar way and will set a standard for financial statements.

Definition, Purpose and Scope of Space Accounting

Space accounting can be considered as the expertise needed to harmonize space activities and accounting practices and to solve possible problems in that accounting. It will be a requirement for governments and commercial enterprises investing in this field.

Space discoveries are the profound transformation of people and society in all aspects. This transformation provides a point of intersection between science and engineering practice. Developments in space change both accounting application processes and required skill sets. In this way, it creates a need for a new kind of accounting expertise that will support the decision-making processes of institutions and society.

Space accounting expertise focuses on economic transactions in space and has both macro and micro scale fields of applications. It covers asteroid mining and space tourism, and any other part of the space exploration budget that will affect the accounting profession.

Space accounting experts should be in a position to closely follow developments in space. This will make it possible for them to report and categorize costs and expenses in the space industry accurately and effectively. Then they will have the tools to help institutions manage their space exploration and space-related investments.

Space accounting expertise will ensure that space activities are expressed in numbers, and that they are analyzed and interpreted together with other data, to then transform them into comparable information to manage space exploration properly and solve any accounting problems that arise. This will help them to provide guidance to relevant institutions and stakeholders in their decisions. Strategies to be created for sustainable space activities are aimed at information based on the mutual interactions that exist between economy and accounting. The main purpose of space accounting expertise is to present space discoveries and economic data together and in a comparable way, observing the aim of sustainability.

Space accounting can be defined as follows: "It is the sub-expertise branch of accounting that enables the establishment of accounting standards and information systems to document and report all economic activities that occur during exploration, research, understanding, management, and use of space as well as the functional activities that are carried out in this field to ensure that organizations make informed decisions about space activities and to ensure sustainability." Considering the rapidly growing space research and economy, space accounting expertise may be among the top jobs in demand in the future.

The general objective of the profession is to produce information and try to explain the interaction between this produced information, space activities, and the economy as a whole. Space accounting is a perfect catalyst for space exploration and the growth of the space industry. It is used to record, summarize, and report the financial transactions of businesses in space in a given reporting period and is a way of calculating industrial activities in space.

Of course, this expertise will also enable integrated reporting that takes into account the non-financial data of enterprises along with their financial data. This integrated reporting can be used to describe their status within the framework of sustainability. In addition to all of these, it will be able to provide tools such as charts of accounts, analysis, presentation, and valuation techniques that will help concerned persons to not only calculate and record economic values in space, but also to make the right decisions about the correct and effective use of resources in space. As can be understood from the above statements, the starting point is to record space discoveries in accordance with accounting principles and to report the obtained information to interest groups in an accurate, impartial, honest, appropriate, and timely manner. For this reason, it directly supports the space explorations and actions of countries and companies.

In the light of all these assessments, the general framework of space accounting can be identified as follows:

- Space accounting is a derivative of accounting.
- Space accounting is the expertise developed to harmonize space activities with accounting practices and to solve possible problems.
- Space accounting focuses on economic operations in space and has both macro and micro scale application areas.
- Some may predict this accounting practice to be more complex than conventional accounting practices. (I do not agree with this; who or what will determine the relevant complexity? Such a generalization is not appropriate since everyone's perception level is different.)
- It covers space and asteroid mining as well as how space exploration spending will affect accounting practices and information systems.
- By means of space accounting, it will be possible to track, report, and categorize costs and other expenditures in the space industry accurately and effectively.
- It will help institutions to manage their space explorations and space-related investments accurately and effectively.
- To ensure the sound management of space explorations and solve

the resulting accounting problems at this point, space accounting expertise will strive to express the space activities in numbers, interpret and analyze them together with other non-financial data and transform them into comparable information, and thereby providing guidance to the relevant institutions and stakeholders in their decisions.

Discussion and Conclusion

Space discoveries will transform the lives of individual people and society profoundly in all aspects. This transformation provides a point of intersection between science and engineering practice. Global space research builds the infrastructure of many modern technologies of our age, and it also directly affects the accounting profession and opens the door to new accounting practices. Developments in space change both the accounting application processes and the required skill sets. Strategies to be created for sustainable space activities are aimed at information based on the mutual interactions that exist between economy and accounting. The main purpose of space accounting expertise is to present space discoveries and economic data together and in a comparable way, observing the aim of sustainability.

How will the accounting records of economic activities in space be, and in which accounts will the income and assets be followed? Which methods and principles will be used in costing operations? How will taxation be done? Will the sector have measurement and value units specific to it or even its own new monetary unit in the form of space currency? Is it necessary to establish unions or organizations such as chambers of commerce or industry for issues such as starting work at various stages of space activities, permits, authorizations, classification, restrictions, inspection, and surveillance? How and by whom will the decisions and arrangements about the structure of these organizations be made? Many more questions can be added to all those given above in order to create a reasonable thought and discussion ground about space accounting.

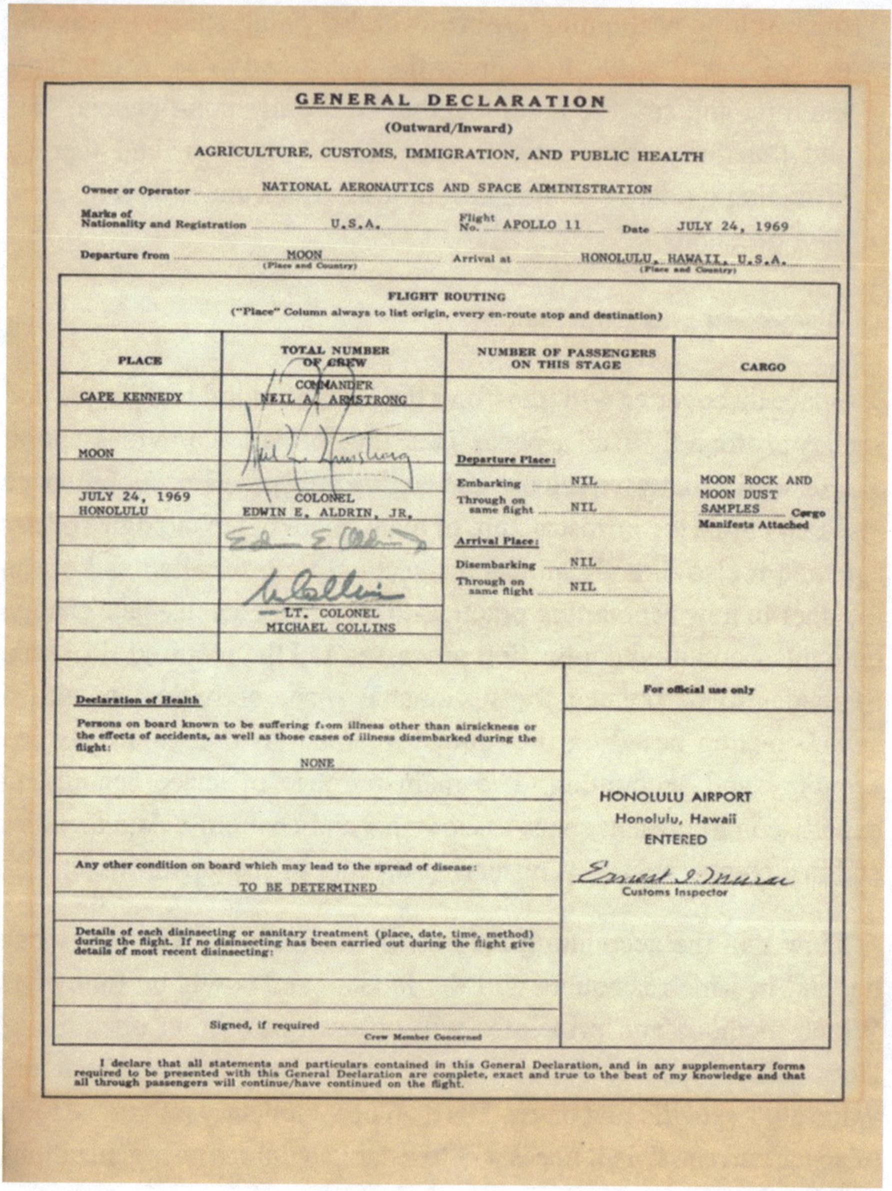

GENERAL DECLARATION

(Outward/Inward)

AGRICULTURE, CUSTOMS, IMMIGRATION, AND PUBLIC HEALTH

Owner or Operator NATIONAL AERONAUTICS AND SPACE ADMINISTRATION

Marks of Nationality and Registration U.S.A. Flight No. APOLLO 11 Date JULY 24, 1969

Departure from MOON (Place and Country) Arrival at HONOLULU, HAWAII, U.S.A. (Place and Country)

FLIGHT ROUTING

("Place" Column always to list origin, every en-route stop and destination)

PLACE	TOTAL NUMBER OF CREW	NUMBER OF PASSENGERS ON THIS STAGE	CARGO
CAPE KENNEDY MOON JULY 24, 1969 HONOLULU	COMMANDER NEIL A. ARMSTRONG *Neil A. Armstrong* COLONEL EDWIN E. ALDRIN, JR. *Edwin E. Aldrin* *M. Collins* LT. COLONEL MICHAEL COLLINS	Departure Place: Embarking NIL Through on same flight NIL Arrival Place: Disembarking NIL Through on same flight NIL	MOON ROCK AND MOON DUST SAMPLES Cargo Manifests Attached

Declaration of Health

Persons on board known to be suffering from illness other than airsickness or the effects of accidents, as well as those cases of illness disembarked during the flight:

NONE

Any other condition on board which may lead to the spread of disease:

TO BE DETERMINED

Details of each disinsecting or sanitary treatment (place, date, time, method) during the flight. If no disinsecting has been carried out during the flight give details of most recent disinsecting:

Signed, if required
Crew Member Concerned

For official use only

HONOLULU AIRPORT
Honolulu, Hawaii
ENTERED
Ernest J. Muraa
Customs Inspector

I declare that all statements and particulars contained in this General Declaration, and in any supplementary forms required to be presented with this General Declaration are complete, exact and true to the best of my knowledge and that all through passengers will continue/have continued on the flight.

A copy of the U.S. Customs form filled out by Apollo 11 astronauts Neil Armstrong, Buzz Aldrin, and Michael Collins after their return to Earth on July 24, 1969. (Image credit: NASA/U.S. Customs and Border Patrol.)[56]

56 https://www.space.com/7044-moon-apollo-astronauts-customs.html

As one example, the Houston-based company Orion Span is planning to build the first luxury hotel in space by late 2021. It will be necessary to establish a set of rules that determine with what values the financial events and transactions that are considered to take place in space will be recorded, how they will be classified, and with which reports they will be presented, such as the depreciation method for the assets of this hotel, valuation, and costing methods of the stocks.

The following recommendations can be developed, so that the space accounting – proposed as a new field of expertise – can function effectively and provide benefits:

- There will be a need for an expert authority that ensures integrity and uniformity by considering the properties specific to space when providing solutions to key problems – such as the technological infrastructure, contracts and human resources, currency to be used, valuation methods, international agreements, costing models, auditing, skill sets, taxation, sustainability, and integrated reporting (which are assumed to constitute the scope of space accounting).
- International Accounting Standards will need to provide a system of rules and principles that determine the format and content of financial statements. These standards should cover how to account for stocks in space, depreciation, research and development costs, income taxes, investments, and tangible and intangible assets. An effective, understandable, and applicable set of space accounting standards will provide significant added value to businesses operating in space and the countries these businesses belong to.
- As accounting is a system that records and reports actual and existing financial transactions and events, one might ask how accountants can form an opinion on an event that has not yet happened. However, it will be necessary to understand and interpret space activities based on expected scenarios and adapt them in accordance with regulated accounting processes. For this purpose, we need working groups that can create the necessary simulations, projections, and models to bring the complex economic activities in space closer to reality. These working groups should include personnel with the appropriate knowledge,

experience, and competence to discuss and investigate topics such as space tourism, space life, space production, asteroid mining, and space discoveries, and could be referred to as **"space accounting experts"**. The authority responsible for inspecting the activities of these working groups, and for the selection and authorization of the people assigned to them, could be called the **"International Space Accounting Standards Board"**. In this way, it will be possible for accounting science to follow and analyze more closely the economic developments in space, such as engineering, astronomy, and physical sciences, so that the relevant accounting science will be fully established by the time the related field of business starts to operate.

• Space accounting experts will be expected to know the terms, concepts, measurements, weights, and calculations used in space activities pertaining to this field and have the competence to manage each process. In this context, internationally recognized professional competency certified programs in space accounting should be organized for space accounting professionals. When determining the certificate education program, science branches or disciplines such as physics, biology, mathematics, engineering, and internet and information technologies should also be utilized in order to provide the satisfactory skills required for space research.

• Considering that money and all monetary concepts will eventually pass-through accounting science, space accounting can be proposed as an interdisciplinary field of study based on spatial, social, and temporal relations at the intersection of sciences such as economics, physics, psychology, geography, architecture, engineering, philosophy, history, and sociology. Undoubtedly, experts working in accounting science will be able to find answers to the problems related to space with an interdisciplinary approach by making use of the branches of science mentioned above.

• In conclusion, just as the accounting practices and reporting of companies doing international business are conceptualized by being placed in certain contexts over time, it will become a prerequisite for the companies conducting business in space to have the revenues they gain or costs they incur accounted for, presented in financial tables, and subjected to taxation. Considering current developments and increasing technological capabilities, it is necessary to carry out studies in the field of space accounting, to establish teams to carry out these studies, and to take critical precautions to avoid falling behind the innovations of the age.

V.1-CHRONOLOGY OF THE AUTHOR'S STUDIES CONDUCTED ON SPACE ACCOUNTING

The concept of "space accounting" was first mentioned in the author's book, "Digital Transformation of Accounting and Accounting Engineering", published in March 2019, in the chapter titled "Accounting Industry in 2050". Later, this chapter was published in Harvard Business Review Turkey under the title of "New Age of Accounting Industry: Space Accounting". The paper titled "A New Accounting Expertise Proposal in Line with Developments in Space: Space Accounting", prepared by the author together with Prof. Dr. Murat Azaltun, Assoc. Dr. Ersin Kurnaz and Certified Public Accountant Arzu Aktas, was approved and published at the International Accounting and Finance Research Congress held in Nigde between October 23-25, 2019. The author's article titled Science Fiction or the Future: Space Accounting was published on the Spacemag Turkey website on December 5, 2019. In 2019, all due registrations of the concept of "space accounting" were made in relevant institutions, including the Ministry of Culture and the Trademark Patent Institute in Turkey. The author plans to continue his research on the concept of "space accounting" within the scope of his doctoral education in the future years.

ICAFR'19

6th INTERNATIONAL CONGRESS ON ACCOUNTING AND FINANCE RESEARCH

24-25 OCTOBER 2019

NİĞDE ÖMER HALİSDEMİR UNIVERSITY – NİĞDE / TURKEY

LETTER OF ACCEPTANCE

25.07.2019

Dear İsmil TEKBAŞ, Dr. Ersin KURNAZ, Prof. Dr. Murat AZALTUN, Arzu AKTAŞ,

The abstract of your paper entitled ***"A NEW ACCOUNTING EXPERTISE PROPOSAL IN ACCORDANCE WITH DEVELOPMENTS IN THE SPACE: SPACE ACCOUNTING"*** *was accepted for a 15 minutes oral presentation at the 6th International Congress on Accounting and Finance Research which will be held on 24-25 October 2019 in Niğde Ömer Halisdemir University – Niğde / Turkey.*

Thank you for your interest in the International Congress on Accounting and Finance Research.

Prof. Dr. Ahmet Vecdi CAN
Congress Coordinator

"Space Accounting" paper was presented for the first time at the 4th International Accounting and Finance Research Congress held on 23 October – 25 October 2019 in Nigde.

The Profession of the Digital Age: Accounting Engineering

Ismail Tekbas | September 5, 2018 |

In the twenty-first century, it is possible to see the footsteps of digitalization at almost every intersection of social life. Digital technology: it affects almost all aspects of modern life from individuals to societies, from economies to cultures—and changes the world. Rapidly changing technological, economic and thinking means professions are forced to change according to the world order, and professional organizations are looking for new approach models. In today's world, digitalization for professions has become a necessity rather than a choice. Professions that do not comply with technological changes will undoubtedly take their places on dusty pages of history.

As it is in other professions, the accountancy profession is also changing and developing as a result of digitization and technological developments. Thanks to computer systems, the workload of accountants has been reduced; complicated and difficult accounting transactions made using traditional methods are made easily and quickly. In accountancy's future, the need for digitalization and transformation is imperative. Traditional accounting methods (such as paper, receipts, registration, declaration, notification, etc.) will eventually go, and all will be done by internet-based accounting systems (such as cloud system and blockchain technology). Against this unabated rise of digitalization, is the accounting industry ready for this revolution?

The Future of the Accountancy Profession in Light of Digitalization

The Fourth Industrial Revolution, triggered by digital technologies, is now pointing to the transformation of the economy and society, depending on developments in artificial intelligence, robotics, autonomous devices, 3D printers, nanotechnology and other areas of science. These developments will change our ways of doing business, and will change us and society as human beings. It is estimated that some professions will disappear completely, some will develop more, and the branches of professions that we have never known today will emerge. As a result of all developments, it is inevitable that these systems will (and are) influence accountancy.

The effects of artificial intelligence, blockchain technology, the Fourth Industrial Revolution and cloud system software on the future of accountancy are being talked about and discussed. Questions like, "What new opportunities will these systems create in accountancy?", "How will digitalization and technology affect the accountancy profession and professionals?", and "Is the accountancy profession and professionals ready to change?" are being asked and discussed in the accounting industry.

Technological developments, globalization, and increasing competition force professions to change constantly. Undoubtedly, the accountancy profession is at the forefront of professions that are most affected by technological developments and globalization. The technology revolution experienced by the accountancy profession was sudden and rapid. With technological developments, many digital systems that did not exist ten years ago are now actively used in the accountancy profession.

In the coming years, many transactions made by accountants will be made by artificial intelligence and automation systems. Day after day, business owners will start looking for more technological talent in accountants, and in the future half-time virtual accountants will emerge instead of full-time accountants. It is an unquestionable fact that the language of the next generation of accountancy professionals will be digitalization and technology.

In the 21st century, the accountancy profession needs a new model able to respond to technological changes and developments in the process of digitalization and e-transformation so that the accounting profession is more effective. In light of technological developments and changes, this modeling should prepare the accountancy profession for the future by rebuilding from A to Z in fields such as thought, education, culture, and technology.

I believe this transformation can only happen with engineering abilities. The solution at this point is "Accounting Engineering," which will enable the accounting profession to evolve with engineering abilities. What is accounting engineering? Accounting Engineering is the redesign of the accountancy profession in light of technological developments, such as digitalization, artificial intelligence, and the Fourth Industrial Revolution.

The Relationship between Accounting and Engineering

In accounting and engineering, there is the need to collect, analyze, develop and action solutions and report to decision makers. Both disciplines act by input-process-output facts, that is, a system approach. Today, in parallel with the developments in technology, accounting and engineering have become more closely related. Engineering science is a science that will enable the accountancy profession to integrate with technological developments by understanding the traditional and variable structure of the accountancy profession.

Engineering science will provide accountants analytical and numerical thinking, effective communication, problem solving, digitalization adaptation, creativity and the ability to look at events from the big picture. Undoubtedly, one of the most important influences of the engineering profession in the accountancy profession is its approach to scientific management.

Scientific management is a theory that analyzes and synthesizes workflows. Scientific management is the application of scientific methods to problems. The use of scientific methods instead of traditional methods in accounting processes will increase the efficiency and the speed.

Engineering is a system of thought and a mathematical thinking skill. Engineering can find new ideas for industry and technology, and manage those ideas. It can change the living conditions of humankind with ideas that create change. An engineering career has become very different nowadays. Beyond designing and constructing, engineers deal with complex social issues, such as poverty, inequality, disaster recovery or climate change. For example, social engineering, environmental engineering, change engineering and risk engineering.

Financial engineering is born in the light of this vision. Today, the weaknesses in the practice of the accountancy profession are more than strengths. Rapidly developing technological and digital developments reveal the need for change in the accounting profession in order to solve the problems that can be defined as weaknesses. In the 21st century, accountants who are trained as accounting engineers or who develop themselves in engineering subjects will be preferred because the accounting profession is no longer the traditional way of working and has turned toward smart technologies.

Engineering skills will enhance accountants' ability to use and manage technology. Accounting Engineering will enable accountants to use the different digital systems to acquire the right knowledge and to manage and use technology in the learning-teaching process. An accounting engineer is a person who can adapt to technological developments and actively use technological products in professional practices, specialized in his own field, combine practical and theoretical knowledge with philosophy, mathematics, and technology.

As a result, recognizing devastating technologies and managing digital systems effectively is of critical importance for the accountancy profession's future. The emergence of new accounting systems as a result of technological change is not distant. In order to prepare the accountancy profession for the future, Accounting Engineering is redesigning the profession within the framework of engineering ability.

The author's article titled "The Profession of the Digital Age: Accounting Engineering" was published by International Federation of Accountants (IFAC) on September 5th, 2018.

This book is an expanded version of the author's thesis "A Research on the Effects of Digitalization on the Accounting Profession and Members of the Profession and a New Concept Proposal: Accounting Engineering", prepared within the scope of Okan University's Accounting and Auditing Program in 2018. Details of the references can be accessed at https://tez.yok.gov.tr/UlusalTezMerkezi/.

Research on the book took about five years. Hundreds of sources were used in this study. All sources are included in the "References" section of the book. The studies that are omitted in the references will be added in the future editions, if found.

REFERENCES

Books:

[1] Ford M., (2015)., ***Robotlarin Yukselisi, Nisan 2018,*** Kronik Kitap, Istanbul

[2] Harari, Y. N., & Genc, E. (2015)., **Hayvanlardan Tanrilara: Sapiens: Insan Turunun Kisa Bir Tarihi**. Kolektif.

[3]Richard S., Danil S., (2015)., ***"The Future of The Professions"***

[4]Rogers David., (2016)., ***"The Digital Transformation Playbook"*** Columbia University Press

[5]Lazol, I., Gursoy Y., (2006)., ***Bilgisayarli Muhasebe I-II,*** Ekin Kitapevi, Bursa.

[6]Lev B., Gu F., (2016)., ***"The End of Accounting and the Path Forward for Investors and Managers"***

[7] Young, M. R., (2002), ***Accounting Irregularities and Financial Fraud, A Corporate Governance Guide***, Second Edition, Aspen Law & Businiess, New York.

[8] Kalayci, S., (Ed.)., (2010), ***SPSS Uygulamali Cok Degiskenli Istatistik Teknikleri,*** 5. Baski, Detay Yayincilik, Ankara.

[9]BASALLA, G. (2013), ***Teknolojinin Evrimi,*** C. Soydemir (Cev.) Ankara: Dogu-Bati

[10]WorldCom (Firm). Board of Directors. Special Investigative Committee, Beresford, D. R., Katzenbach, N. D., & Rogers, C. B. (2003). Report of investigation. Findlaw.

[11]Muller, H., (2020***) Future State 2025: How Top Technology Executives Disrupt and Drive Success in the Digital Economy***

[12]Fingar, C. T. (Ed.). (2009). ***Global trends 2025: A transformed world*** DIANE Publishing.

[13]Dibbern, J., & Hirschheim, R. (2020). ***Introduction: Riding the waves of outsourcing change in the era of digital transformation***. In Information Systems Outsourcing (pp. 1-20). Springer, Cham.

Theses:

[1]Aslan, M., (2015), ***Tarihsel Surec Icerisinde Turkiye'de Kullanilan Muhasebe Sistemleri ve Iktisadi Devlet Tesekkulleri Uzerinden Ornekler***, Doktora Tezi, Canakkale Onsekiz Mart Universitesi Sosyal Bilimler Enstitusu Isletme Anabilim Dali,

Canakkale, Turkiye.

[2]Bayraktar, M. E., (2010), ***Kullanici Hareketleriyle Mekân Kurgusu: Etmen Tabanli Bir Tasarim Araci,*** Yuksek Lisans Tezi, Istanbul Teknik Universitesi Fen Bilimleri Enstitusu, Istanbul, Turkiye.

[3]Cakal, H., (2016), ***Modernlesme Baglaminda Osmanli Muhasebe Sistemindeki Degisim,*** Yuksek Lisans Tezi, Okan Universitesi Sosyal Bilimler Enstitusu, Istanbul, Turkiye.

[4]Guzel, M., (2010), ***Muhasebenin Tarihcesi ve Gelisimi,*** Yuksek Lisans Tezi, Breyer State University Business Administration, Istanbul, Turkiye.

[5]Uysal D. Y., (2009), ***Bilgi Teknolojileri Yatirimlari, Bilgi Teknolojileri Performansi ve Karar Verme Iliskisi Uzerine Bir Arastirma,*** Yuksek Lisans Tezi, Istanbul Universitesi Sosyal Bilimler Enstitusu, Istanbul, Turkiye.

[6]Zengin, H., (2016), ***Muhasebe Mesleginde Meslek Mensubunun Problemleri ve Muhasebe Denetiminde Karsilasilan Hileler,*** *Meslek Mensubunun Tutumu,* Yuksel Lisans Tezi, Okan Universitesi Sosyal Bilimler Enstitusu, Istanbul, Turkiye.

Articles:

[1]Sevim, A., Bulbul, S., (2017), ***Bilgi Teknolojisi (BT) Projelerinin Basarisinda Muhasebe Bilgi Sisteminin (MBS) Rolu ve Muhasebecinin Katkilari,*** Balkan Sosyal Bilimler Dergisi, 2017, 6. Cilt, Sayi: 11, s. 1-18.

[2]Akgul, A., Ucar, M. K., Ozturk, M. M., Eksi, Z., (2013), ***Muhendislik Egitiminin Iyilestirilmesine Yonelik Oneriler, Gelecegin Muhendisleri ve Isgucu Analizi,*** Suleyman Demirel Universitesi Fen Bilimleri Enstitusu Dergisi, 17. Cilt, Sayi: 1, s. 14-18.

[3]Akgun A. I., Kilic S., (2013), ***Muhasebe Bilgi Sisteminin Isletme Yonetiminin Etkinligi Uzerindeki Etkisi,*** Yonetim ve Ekonomi Dergisi, Cilt 20, Sayi: 2, s. 21-36.

[4]Aktan, C.C., Tunc, M., (1998), ***Bilgi Toplumu ve Egitim,*** Yeni Turkiye Dergisi, 21. Yuzyil Özel Sayisi, 4(19), s. 118-133.

[5]Alpaslan, N., (2011), ***Muhendislik Tarihi ve Felsefesi Uzerine Bir Arastirma,*** Marmara Sosyal Arastirmalar Dergisi, Sayi: 1, s. 1-10.

[6]Aslan, U., Özerhan, Y., (2017), ***Big Data, Muhasebe ve Muhasebe meslegi,*** Muhasebe Bilim Dunyasi Dergisi, Aralik 2017,

19(4), s. 862-883.

[6]Ayanoglu, Y., Zaif, F., (2007), ***Muhasebe Egitiminde Kalitenin Arttirilmasinda Ders Programlarinin Önemi Turkiye'de Bir Inceleme,*** Gazi universitesi Iktisadi ve Idari Bilimler Fakultesi Dergisi, 9/1, s. 115-136.

[7]Aydemir, O., (2015), ***Muhasebe Meslek Mensuplarinin Karsilastiklari Sorunlar ve Beklentiler,*** Muhasebe ve Finansman Dergisi, Temmuz, s. 71-84.

[8] Aysan A. M., (2006) ***Turkiye'de Muhasebe Mesleginin Gelisimi,*** Istanbul Serbest Muhasebeci Mali Musavirler Odasi Mali Cozum Dergisi, Kasim, Sayi: 76, s. 32-41.

[9]Banar, K. Ekergil, V., (2010)., ***Muhasebe Meslek Mensuplarinin Hizmet Kalitesi: Sunulan Hizmetlerin Kalitesi ile Musteri Memnuniyeti Iliskisi: Eskisehir Uygulamasi,*** Anadolu Universitesi Sosyal Bilimler Dergisi, Cilt:10 Sayi:1, s. 39–60.

[11]Bendovschi, A., C., (2015), ***The Evolution of Accounting Information Systems,*** Bucharest University of Economics Bucharets Romania SEA Practical Application of Science Volume III, Issue 1 (7), s. 91-95.

[12]Bicer, A. A., Akarcay V., Mulkut U., (2017), ***Etik Degerlerin Muhasebe Mesleginin Itibari Uzerindeki Rolu,*** Istanbul Ticaret Universitesi Sosyal Bilimler Dergisi, Yil: 16, Sayi: 31, Bahar, s. 197-206.

[13]Cenikli E., Sahin, D., (2013), ***Turk Gelir Idaresinde Otomasyon Projeleri,*** Internet Uygulamalari ve Yonetim Dergisi, IUYD. 4 (1), s. 37-52

[14]Deran, A., Erduru I., Keles, D., (2016), ***Muhasebe Meslek Mensuplarinin Mesleki Sorunlari ve Meslek Odalarindan Beklentilerinin Demografik Özellikler ve Faaliyet Gosterilen Ekonomik Cevre Acisindan Degerlendirilmesi: Ordu Örnegi,*** Selcuk Universitesi Iktisadi ve Idari Bilimler Fakultesi Sosyal Ekonomik Arastirmalar Dergisi, Sayi: 16(32), s. 84-109.

[15]Demir, B., (2012), ***Muhasebeye Yon Veren Gelismeler ve Meslek Yuksekokullarinda Verilen Muhasebe Egitimine Yansimalari,*** Egitim ve Ögretim Arastirmalari Dergisi, Kasim, Cilt 1, Sayi 4, s. 109-120.

[16]Dizman, S., Guney, S., (2015), ***Muhasebe Meslek Mensuplarinin Sorunlari Kamuda Karsilasilan Olumsuzluklar ve Beklentiler (Erzincan Ili Uygulamasi),*** Akademik Sosyal

Arastirmalar Dergisi, 2915, S: 3(16), s. 97-110.

[17]Erturan, E. I., Emre, E., (2018), ***Muhasebe Mesleginde Dijitallesme: Endustri 4.0 Etkisi,*** Akademik Sosyal Arastirmalar Dergisi, Yil:6, S: 72, Haziran 2018 s. 34-42.

[18]Can A.V., (2007), ***Luca Pacioli Muhasebenin Babasi midir?*** Uluslararasi Hakemli Sosyal Bilimler E-Dergisi, Sayi 12, Mayis, s. 2-15.

[19]Cabuk A., Saygili A.T., (2013), ***Osmanli Imparatorlugu'nda XIX. Yuzyilin Ortalarinda Devlet Muhasebesinde Merdiven Yonteminde Cift Yanli Kayit Yontemine Gecis,*** Muhasebe ve Finans Tarihi Arastirmalari Dergisi, Sayi 4 Ocak-Subat, s. 168-196.

[20]Figen Z. F., Ayanoglu, Y., (2007), ***Muhasebe Egitiminde Kalitenin Arttirilmasinda Ders Programlarinin Önemi: Turkiye'de Bir Inceleme,*** Gazi Universitesi Iktisadi ve Idari Bilimler Fakultesi Dergisi, 9/1, s. 115-136.

[21]Gencoglu, M. T., Gencoglu E., (2005'a), ***Muhendislik Egitiminde Yeni Yaklasimlar,*** Kaynak Elektrik, Sayi: 195, s. 89-93.

[22]Gokgoz, A., (2010-2011) ***Tarihsel Perspektifte Muhasebenin Dogusunu ve Gelisimini Etkileyen Faktorler,*** Yalova Sosyal Bilimler Dergisi, Sayi:1 Ekim- Mart, s. 167 177.

[23]Gokgoz, A., Zeytin M., (2012), ***Muhasebe Meslek Mensuplarinin Mesleki Faaliyetlerinde Karsilastiklari Sorunlar ve Beklentileri: Bilecik ve Yalova Illeri Uygulamasi,*** Suleyman Demirel Universitesi Iktisadi ve Idari Bilimler Fakultesi Dergisi, S: 17(1), s. 477-493.

[24]Guney, S., Mutlu, S., (2008) ***Bilgi Teknolojilerinin Girisimcilige Etkileri,*** COMU Dergileri Girisimcilik ve Kalkinma Dergisi, Cilt: 3, Sayi: 1, s. 85-99.

[25]Guvemli, O., Aytulun, A., Sisman, B., (2013) ***Turkiye'de Muhasebe Mesleginin Gelismesi ve Ilk Meslek Orgutlenmesi: Turkiye Muhasebe Uzmanlari Dernegi – 1942,*** Muhasebe ve Finans Tarihi Arastirmalar Dergisi, Sayi 4, s. 19-49.

[26]Karakas, M. S., Calik, A., ***Muhendislik Egitiminde Disiplinler Arasi Yaklasimlar,*** Mustafa Suleyman Demirel Universitesi Fen Bilimleri Enstitusu Dergisi, 17(1), s. 45-49.

[27]Kaya, G. A., (2015) ***Muhasebe Meslek Mensuplarinin Sorunlari ve Cozum Önerileri: Elazig'da Bir Arastirma,*** The Journal of Academic Social Science Studies, S: 41, s. 207-231.

[28]Miman, M., Yogun A, E., Önel, E., (2016), ***Yonetim Bilgi***

Sistemleri Kullanim Ozellikleri Arasindaki Iliskiler: Lojistik Sektoru Uzerine Bir Calisma, Akademik Bakis Dergisi, Mart-Nisan, Sayi: 54, s. 161-173.

[29]Sayim, F., Usman, O., (2016), ***Muhasebe Meslegi Icin Mesleki Durum Analizi Kriterlerinin Belirlenmesi,*** Yalova Sosyal Bilimler Dergisi, Sayi: 7(12), s. 105-122.

[30]Seethamraju, R., (2010), **Information Technologies in Accounting Education**, The University of Sydney, Australi

[31]Oldroyd, David (1995) **"Role of accounting in public expenditure and monetary policy in the first century AD Roman Empire,"** *Accounting Historians Journal*: Vol. 22: Iss. 2, Article 5.

[30]Öz, Y., (2016), ***Bulut Bilisim (Cloud Computing) ve Muhasebe,*** Bartin Universitesi I.I.B.F. Dergisi, Sayi: 7(13), s. 63-79.

[31] Özturk, Z. B., Kacmaz H., Cirik, R., Turkyilmaz, M., (2015), ***Muhendislik Etigi ve Turkiye'de Metalurji-Malzeme Muhendisligi Bolumunun Etik Acidan Degerlendirilmesi,*** Nevsehir Bilim ve Teknoloji Dergisi, Sayi:4(1), s. 81-87. Doi:10.17100/nevbiltek.210939.

[32]Özyurek, H. (2012), ***Muhasebe Meslek Mensuplarinin Tasimasi Gereken Nitelikler,*** Hukuk ve Iktisat Arastirmalari Dergisi Cilt 4, No 1, s. 139-14.

[33]Pekdemir R., Önal M. M., (1999), ***Bilgi Teknolojisindeki Gelismelerin Muhasebe Meslegine Etkileri,*** Yonetim Dergisi, Yil 10, Sayi 34 Ekim, s.7-14.

[34]Uzay S., (2004), ***21. Yuzyilin Basinda Muhasebe Meslegini Etkileyen Gelismeler ve Gelecege Yonelik Degerlendirmeler,*** Istanbul Serbest Muhasebeci Mali Musavirler Odasi Mali Cozum Dergisi, Sayi: 67, s. 230-237.

[35]Sayar, Z., Karatas, M., (2017), ***Muhasebe ve Denetim Alaninda Yasanan Son Gelismeler ile Muhasebe Mesleginde Yeni Trendler,*** ISMMMO Mali Cozum Dergisi, Ocak-Subat, s. 13-27.

[36]Sayim F., Usman., O., (2016), ***Muhasebe Meslegi Icin Mesleki Durum Analizi Kriterlerinin Belirlenmesi,*** Yalova Sosyal Bilimler Dergisi, Yil: 7, Sayi: 12, s. 105-122.

[37]Terzi, A., (2015), ***Muhasebe Meslek Mensuplarinin Meslekleri ile Ilgili Beklentilerine, Sorunlarina ve Algilarina Yonelik Bir Arastirma: Rize Örnegi,*** Ardahan Universitesi Iktisadi ve Idari Bilimler Fakultesi Dergisi, Sayi: 2, s. 193-212.

[38]Tugay, O., Teksen, O., (2014), ***Muhasebe Meslek***

Mensuplarinin Sorunlari: Burdur Ilinde Bir Arastirma, Suleyman Demirel Universitesi Iktisadi ve Idari Bilimler Fakultesi Dergisi, Sayi:19(1), s. 223-232.

[39]Walker Stephen P., Tercume Aslan, U, (2011) ***Muhasebe Tarihi Arastirmalarinda Arastirma ve Yazma,*** Muhasebe ve Finans Arastirmalari Dergisi, Sayi 1, s.17-23.

[40]Yildirim, S., Guney, S., (2012), ***Serbest Muhasebeci Mali Musavirlerin Genel Sorunlari: Erzurum Ili Örnegi,*** Muhasebe ve Denetime Bakis, 4, s. 35-48.

[41]Yukcu, S., Atagan G., (2010*),* ***Muhasebenin Muhendislik Boyutu: Urun Agaci ve Rota Uygulamasi,*** Mali Cozum Dergisi, Kasim-Aralik, s. 21-38.

[42]BADUA, F. A., and Watkins, A. L. (2011), ***Too Young to Have a History. Using Data Analysis Techniques to Reveal Trends and Shifts in the Brief History of Accounting Information Systems,*** *Accounting Historians Journal*, 38(2), 75-103.

[43]BREY, P. (2008), ***Technological Design as an Evolutionary Process***. "Eds. Vermaas, P., Kroes, P., Light, A. and Moore, S. Philosophy and Design: From Engineering to Architecture. Springer. 22 pp.

[44]CANKOCAK, K. (2009), ***Evrenin Evrimi Kuarklarin Kendiliginden Macerasinda Simetri ve Simetri Kirinimi***, Cogito Yapi Kredi Yayinlari-Uc Aylik Dusunce Dergisi s. 60-61.

[45]Soll, J. (2014). The vanished grandeur of accounting: Once, bookkeepers were valorized in great art. Sound funny now? The joke might be on us. The Boston Globe, 8.

[46]VASILEV, J. ***The change from ERP II to ERP III systems***, Conference Paper July 2014 (3rd International Conference on Application of Information and Communication Technology and Statistics in Economy and Education (ICAICTSEE 2013), At Sofi)

[47]MARAKAS, G. (2012), O'Brien, James. ***Introduction to Information Systems***, 16th Ed. New York: Irwin/McGrawHill.

[48]Frey, C. B., & Osborne, M. A. (2017). ***The future of employment: How susceptible are jobs to computerisation? Technological forecasting and social change***, 114, 254-280.

[49]Warwick, K., & Shah, H. (2016). ***Can machines think? A report on Turing test experiments at the Royal Society***. Journal of experimental & Theoretical artificial Intelligence, 28(6), 989-1007.

[50]Ozdogan, B. (2017). ***The future of accounting profession in***

an era of start-ups. Accounting and corporate reporting-today and tomorrow.

[51]Willcocks, L., Lacity, M., & Craig, A. (2017). ***Robotic process automation: strategic transformation lever for global business services?*** Journal of Information Technology Teaching Cases, 7(1), 17-28.

[52]Forrest, C. (2015). ***Chinese factory replaces 90% of humans with robots, production soars.*** *Tech Republic.*

[53]KARAER,O.,***MANAGINGARETAILFASHIONPRODUCT WITH RFID-ENABLED INVENTORY VISIBILITY.*** *Nigde Omer Halisdemir Universitesi Muhendislik Bilimleri Dergisi*, *8*(2), 796-809.

[54] Khazzam, R., E., (2015). ***3D Printing Technology Shifts the Cost Modeling Game—What You and Your Clients Need to Know***. IFAC URL: https://www.ifac.org/knowledge-gateway/preparing-future-ready-professionals/discussion/3d-printing-technology-shifts-cost-modeling-game-what-you-and-your-clients-need-know

[55] Lueth, K. L. (2015). ***IoT basics: Getting started with the Internet of Things***. White paper,

[56] Goodwin, T. (2017). ***The battle is for the customer interface*** (2015).

[57] Morgan, B. (2019). ***100 Stats on Digital Transformation and Customer Experience.*** *Forbes.*

[58]Melendez, C. (2016). ***Artificial intelligence gets into auditing, what's next?*** *Infoworld.com.*

[59] Maali, B., & Al-Attar, A. M. (2020). ***Accounting curricula in universities and market needs: The jordanian case.*** *SAGE Open*, *10*(1), 2158244019899463.

[60] Omodeo, P. D. (2016). ***Kuhn's paradigm of paradigms: historical and epistemological coordinates of 'The Copernican revolution'. In Shifting paradigms: Thomas S. Kuhn and the history of science*** (pp. 71-104). Edition Open Access.

[61] Yolac, S., & Dogan, E. (2011). ***Kuresellesme Surecinde Aile Isletmelerinde Yonetim ve Kurumsallasma***. *Istanbul Universitesi Iktisat Fakultesi Mecmuasi*, *61*(2), 83-110.

[62] Abitzsch, S. (1996). ***Prospects of Space Tourism***, 9th European Aerospace Congress – Visions and Limits of Long-term Aerospace Developments. Proceedings of 43 IAF Congress.

http://www.spacefuture.com/archive/prospects_of_space_tourism.shtm

[63] Dormehl, L. (2018). ***Asteroid Mining is Almost Reality. What to Know About the Gold Rush in Space***. https://www.sciencebuddies.org/science-fair-projects/project-ideas/Astro_p038/astronomy/asteroid-mining-gold-rush-in-space

[64] Tekbas, I. (2019) ***Muhasebe Endustrisinin Yeni Cagi: Uzay Muhasebesi*** https://hbrturkiye.com/blog/muhasebe-endustrisinin-yeni-cagi-uzay-muhasebesi

[65] White, F. (2014). ***The Overview Effect: Space Exploration and Human Evolution***. USA: American Institute of Aeronautics and Astronautics.

[66] Ovunda, A. S. (2015). ***Luca Pacioli's Double-Entry System of Accounting: A Critique.*** *Research Journal of Finance and Accounting*, *6*(18), 132-139.

[67]Dodgson, M. (2011). ***Exploring new combinations in innovation and entrepreneurship: social networks, Schumpeter, and the case of Josiah Wedgwood*** (1730–1795). *Industrial and Corporate Change*, *20*(4), 1119-1151.

[68] Lee, T. A. (2013). ***Reflections on the origins of modern accounting***. *Accounting History*, *18*(2), 141-161.

[69] Can, A. V. (2007). ***Luca Pacioli Muhasebenin Babasi midir?*** *Akademik Bakis, Uluslararasi Hakemli Sosyal Bilimler Dergisi*, (12).

Papers/Study of an Organization or a Group:

[1]Allahverdi, M., Karaer, M, (2017), ***Muhasebede E-Donusumun Egitimdeki Yeri ve E-Donusum Egitimi Icin Bir Öneri,*** 36. Muhasebe Egitimi Sempozyumu.

[2]Baser, M. (1999), ***Muhasebe Mesleginin Örgutlenmesinde Turkiye, 4. Turkiye Muhasebe Denetimi Sempozyumu,*** Istanbul Serbest Muhasebeci Mali Musavirler Odasi.

[3]Elmaci, O., Sevim, S., (2015), ***Endustri 4.0 Paradigmasi Cercevesinde Muhasebe Egitiminde Temel Yetenekler ve Stratejik Degerler Nasil Gelistirilir? Kaynak Tabanli Bir Model Onerisi,*** 34. Muhasebe Egitimi Sempozyumu.

[4]Gelir Idaresi Baskanligi., ***(2013,2014 2015,2016,2017), Faaliyet Raporu,*** Strateji Gelistirme Daire Baskanligi.

[5]Firat, H., (2004), ***Globallesmenin Ulkemiz Muhasebe Meslegine Yarattigi Firsatlar,*** Turkiye Muhasebe Denetim Sempozyumu.

[6]Fujinama, A., (2002), ***Globalization and The Role of The Accounting Profession in the 21st Century,*** The 16th World Congress of Accountants, Hong Kong.

[7]Sanli, N. (2014), ***Mesleki Gelismelerle Yasanan Sorunlar, Cozum Yollari ve Hizmet Pazarlamasinin Önemi,*** 9. Turkiye Muhasebe Forumu, TURMOB.

[8]Senol, H., (2016), ***Turkiye'de Muhasebe Alaninda Yasanan E-Donusum Surecine Genel Bir Bakis,*** 3. Uluslararasi Turk Dunyasi Arastirmalari Sempozyumu, Baku.

[9]T.C. Sanayi ve Teknoloji Bakanligi ***"Dijital Turkiye Yol Haritasi Raporu"***

[10]ICAEW ***"Yapay Zeka ve Muhasebenin Gelecegi Raporu"***

[11]***2019 Space Foundation Report*** www.thespacereport.org/pricing

[12]http://www3.weforum.org/docs/WEF_Future_of_Jobs_2020.pdf

Electronic Publications/Internet:

[1]Frey, C. B., Osborne, M. A, (2013), ***The future of employment: how susceptible are jobs to computerisation?*** Alinan adres: ***https://www.oxfordmartin.ox.ac.uk/ downloads/academic/The/Future_of_Employment.pdf,*** Access Date: 18.03.2018.

[2]The Pathways Commission (2015), ***In Pursuit of Accounting's Curricula of the Future, American Accounting Association, http://commons.aaahq.org/,*** Access Date: 05.04.2018.

[3]Tohumoglu, G. (2017), ***Yeni yuzyilin baslarinda nasil bir muhendislik egitimi verilmeli, http://faraday.ee.emu.edu.tr/muhendislik%20Egitimi. pdf,*** Access Date: 26.03.2018.

[4]Deloitte ***(2010) Kuresel Uretim Rekabet Endeksi 2010.*** Access Date 20.Nisan.2018

[5]WEB 1, (2018), ***https://web.hitit.edu.tr/dersnotlari/omurdemirer_24.03.2014 _1D80.pptx,*** Access Date: 17.02.2018.

[6]WEB 2, (2018), ***https://webrazzi.com/2016/10/18/4-sanayi-devrimine-bir-de-yapay-zeka-uzmaninin-gozunden-bakalim/,*** Access Date: 15.05.2018.

[7]WEB 3, (2018), ***https://www.dia.com.tr/bulut-bilisim-muhasebe/?cv=1,*** Access Date: 05.03.2018.

[8]WEB 4, (2018), ***https://home.kpmg.com/content/dam/kpmg/tr/pdf/2016/08/tr-sanayi-4.PDF,*** Access Date: 05.01.2017.

[9]WEB 5, (2018), ***http://ismailtekbas.blogspot.com.tr,*** Access Date: 25.01.2018.

[10]WEB 6, (2018), ***http://www.muhasebetr.com/yazarlarimiz/ismailtekbas/012/,*** Access Date: 05.05.2018.

[11]WEB 7, (2018), ***https://kobiaktuel.com.tr/kobi-aktuel-dosya/aile-sirketlerinin-dagilmasi-bir-kader-mi.html,*** Access Date: 07.01.2018.

[12]WEB 9, (2018), ***https://bilimkafasi.com/deposu-olmayan-market-mi-radyo-frekanslari-sayesinde-her-sey-mumkun/*** Access Date: 10.08.2018.

[13]WEB 10, (2018), ***https://www.dijitaldonusum.gov.tr/*** TUBITAK-BILGEM-YTE Access Date: 18.08.2018.

[14]WEB 9, (2018), ***https://home.kpmg.com/tr/tr/home/insights/2016/09/dijital-isgucu-geliyor-yaklasan-dijital-isgucu-dalgasi.html*** Access Date: 29.10.2018.

[15]WEB 10, (2018), ***https://wearesocial.com/blog/2018/01/global-digital-report-2018 Access Date***: 02.11.2018.

[16]WEB 11, (2018), ***https://www.i-scoop.eu/digital-transformation/*** Access Date: 02.11.2018.

[17]WEB 12, (2018),

http://web.mit.edu/~21fms/People/henry3/pub/digitaltheory Access Date: 10.11.2018.

[18]WEB 13, (2018), ***https://www.careermetis.com/essential-skills-accountants-digital-age/*** Access Date: 11.11.2018.

[19]WEB 14, (2018), ***https://www.hongkiat.com/blog/habits-to-develop-innovative-mind/*** Access Date: 15.11.2018.

[20]WEB 15, (2018),

http://blogs.lse.ac.uk/businessreview/2018/01/17/confronting-the-macroeconomic-challenges-of-the-fourth-industrial-revolution/ Access Date: 23.11.2018.

[21]WEB 16, (2018),

https://www.ncbi.nlm.nih.gov/pmc/articles/PMC5383681/ Access Date: 24.11.2018.

[22]WEB 17, (2018), ***http://file.scirp.org/Html/12-8701198_25200.htm*** Access Date: 28.11.2018.

[23]WEB 18, (2018), ***http://aaapubs.org/doi/full/10.2308/jeta-10494*** Access Date: 28.11.2018.

[25]WEB 20, (2018), ***https://www.bostonglobe.com/ideas/2014/06/07/the-vanished-grandeur-accounting/3zcbRBoPD***

NIryWyNYNMvbO/story.html Access Date: 08.12.2018.

[26]WEB 22, (2018), ***https://www.amerikaninsesi.com/a/a-17-a-2002-06-27-8-1-87863442/797186.html*** Access Date: 14.12.2018.

[27]WEB 23, (2018), ***http://www.offcourse.com.tr/tr/blog/lehman-brothers-dunyanin-en-buyuk-iflasinin-hikayesi*** Access Date: 14.12.2018.

[28]WEB24,(2018),***http://www.hurriyet.com.tr/ik-yeni-ekonomi/bulut-bilisim-130-bin-yeni-is-yaratacak-40956679*** Access Date: 21.12.2018.

[29]WEB 25, (2018), ***https://sldcpa.com/blog/3d-printing-will-shape-future-manufacturing-accounting*** Access Date: 05.01.2019.

[30]WEB 26, (2019), ***https://www.ifac.org/global-knowledge-gateway/business-reporting/discussion/future-accounting-profession-three-major*** Access Date: 10.05.2019.

[31]WEB 27, (2019), ***https://www.newenglandcollegeonline.com/resources/accounting/how-technology-is-changing-the-accounting-profession/*** Access Date: 11.05.2019.

[32]WEB 28, (2019), ***http://www.accountingin.com/accounting-historians-journal/volume-11-number-1/the-significance-of-ancient-mesopotamia-in-accounting-history/ Access Date***: 12.05.2019.

[32]WEB 29, (2019), ***https://futuristspeaker.com/technology-trends/72-stunning-things-in-the-future-that-will-be-common-ten-years-from-now-that-dont-exist-today/*** Access Date: 12.05.2019.

[32]WEB 29, (2019), ***https://www.livescience.com/12916-10-facts-human-brain.html*** Access Date: 12.05.2019.

[32]WEB 30 (2019), ***https://www.dailymail.co.uk/sciencetech/article-3722558/Hackers-inside-BRAIN-Experts-warn-growing-threat-monitoring-controlling-neural-signals.html*** Access Date: 18.05.2019.

[33]WEB 31 (2019), ***http://www.suncorp.com.au/super/grey/your-future/what-will-life-be-2035*** Access Date: 18.05.2019.

[34]WEB 32 (2019), ***https://www.pcmag.com/news/365676/what-tech-will-look-like-in-2039*** Access Date: 18.05.2019.

[34]WEB 33 ***https://www2.deloitte.com/insights/us/en/multimedia/podcasts/navigating-new-forms-of-work.html*** Access Date: 25.05.2019.

[35]WEB 35 ***https://futurism.com/the-next-stage-of-evolution-***

how-will-the-human-species-evolve Access Date: 25.05.2019.

[35]WEB 36 ***https://medium.com/@manuj.aggarwal/technological-advances-and-its-effects-on-human-evolution-5329718639e7*** Access Date: 26.05.2019.

[36]WEB 37 ***https://iedunote.com/accounting-evolution-history*** Access Date: 26.05.2019.

[37]WEB 38 ***https://www.computerweekly.com/feature/Darwinism-theory-of-evolution-applied-to-technology*** Access Date: 28.05.2019.

[38]WEB 39 ***https://scielo.conicyt.cl/scielo.php?script=sci_arttext&pid=S0718-18762015000100001*** Access Date: 26.05.2019.

[38]WEB 39 ***https://www.alternativeaccountancyit.com/sponsor/artificial-intelligence-will-impact-accounting/*** Access Date: 06.06.2019.

[39]WEB 40 ***https://www.pewresearch.org/*** Access Date: 23.06.2019

[39]WEB 40 DEMIR, A. N. (2019), Evrim Teorisine Kisa Bir Bakis, accessed on 04 January 2020 at ***https://www.bezelyedergi.net/post/evrim-teorisine-kisa-bir-bakis***.

[40]Hayes, A., (2019) ***https://www.investopedia.com/articles/investing/020615/20-industries-threatened-tech-disruption.asp*** Access 17.01.2021

[40]***https://www.mckinsey.com/business-functions/mckinsey-digital/our-insights/where-machines-could-replace-humans-and-where-they-cant-yet*** Access 20.01.2021

[41]http://www3.weforum.org/docs/WEF_Future_of_Jobs_2020.pdf_Access 23.01.2021

[42]***https://www.paymentsjournal.com/covid-19-and-accessing-capital-lessons-from-abroad/*** Access 21.01.2021

[43]***https://www.icaew.com/insights/features/2020/may-2020/covid-reveals-the-benefits-of-cloud-working*** Access 21.01.2021

[44]***https://www2.deloitte.com/us/en/pages/financial-services/articles/blockchain-series-deloitte-center-for-financial-services.html/*** Access 24.01.2021

[45]***https://blog.microfocus.com/how-much-data-is-created-on-the-internet-each-day/*** Access 24.01.2021

[46]***https://sldcpa.com/knowledge-insights/3d-printing-will-shape-future-manufacturing-accounting*** Access 24.01.2021

[47]***https://www.accsyssolutions.com/adagio-accounting-***

software/augmented-reality-accounting/ Access 24.01.2021

[47]***https://www.alliedmarketresearch.com/augmented-and-virtual-reality-market*** Access 24.01.2021

[48]***https://www.accountingtoday.com/opinion/virtual-reality-the-new-reality-for-accountants*** Access 24.01.2021

[49]***https://www.bloomaccounting.com.au/is-augmented-reality-the-future-of-accounting/*** Access 24.01.2021

[50]***https://www.ifac.org/news-events/2019-06/tax-trade-and-transparency-dominate-g20-agenda-ifac-issues-call-action*** Access 24.01.2021

[51]***https://cybersecurityventures.com/cybercrime-damage-costs-10-trillion-by-2025/*** Access 25.01.2021

[52]***https://www.varonis.com/blog/cybersecurity-statistics/*** Access 25.01.2021

[54] ***https://www.icaew.com/learning-and-development/aca/aca-employers/the-future-professional*** Access 26.01.2021

[55] ***https://www.mckinsey.com/business-functions/mckinsey-implementation/our-insights/how-the-implementation-of-organizational-change-is-evolving#*** Access 27.01.2021

[56] ***https://www.technologymagazine.com/data-and-data-analytics/mckinsey-unlocking-success-digital-transformations*** Access 27.01.2021

[57] ***https://www.raconteur.net/digital/digital-transformation-failure/*** Access 27.01.2021

[58] ***https://www.thefuturefactory.com/blog/tesla*** Access 27.01.2021

[59] ***https://www.economist.com/business/2019/06/27/will-a-robot-really-take-your-job***

[60] ***https://www.icaew.com/library/historical-resources/female-firsts***

RESUME

Ismail Tekbas was born on January 21, 1984 in the district of Sahinbey of Gaziantep province. He completed his primary and high school education in Gaziantep. He got his associate degree from the Department of Computerized Accounting at the Vocational School of Accounting, University of Gaziantep between 2001-2003, and his undergraduate education at Anadolu University, Faculty of Business Administration, between 2003-2005. Then, he finished his thesis and obtained a master's degree in the Accounting and Auditing Program at Okan University.

Since 2005, he has worked in companies with Turkish and foreign partners, operating in different sectors such as health, recycling, and textile in Gaziantep, among the largest 500 companies in Turkey. He is currently working as a Financial and Administrative Affairs Manager in a private company. Ismail Tekbas is a financial advisor registered in Gaziantep Chamber of Independent Accountants and Financial Advisors with registration number 1544. He conducts research on technologies that affect the future of the accounting profession. His articles on the accounting profession and economics have been published in many national and international journals and websites such as the International Federation of Accountants IFAC, Harvard Business Review Turkey and Investing.com.

He conducted the first academic studies on the concepts of "Accounting Engineering", "Accounting Cultural Centers", "Digital Accounting Literacy" and "Space Accounting" and introduced these concepts to the Turkish and foreign literature. The concept of "Accounting Engineering" was presented to the academic world under the title of "Redesign of the Accounting Profession in the Digital Age: Accounting Engineering" in the 2nd International Thrace Accounting, Finance and Auditing Symposium held on 17-28 October 2017, the concept of "Accounting Cultural Centers" under the title of "Structures That Will Carry Accounting Culture to the Future: Accounting Culture Centers" in the 4th International Accounting and Finance Research Congress held on 14-17 December in Erzurum, the concept of "Digital Accounting Literacy" at the 4th International Symposium on Social Humanities and Administrative Sciences held on 3-5 May 2018 at Alanya Alaaddin Keykubat University, and the concept of "Space Accounting" was presented to the academic world at the 4th International Accounting and Finance Research Congress held on 23 October – 25 October 2019 in Nigde.

The author is currently working on the concept of "Hyper Accounting", which is a new accounting theory in the light of new generation technological developments such as metaverse, Web 3.0 and blockchain.

Made in the USA
Monee, IL
03 November 2026

67391590R10109